101 Best Cover Letters

101 Best Cover Letters

JAY A. BLOCK, CPRW
MICHAEL BETRUS, CPRW

McGraw-Hill
New York   San Francisco   Washington, D.C.   Auckland   Bogotá
Caracas   Lisbon   London   Madrid   Mexico City   Milan
Montreal   New Delhi   San Juan   Singapore
Sydney   Tokyo   Toronto

Library of Congress Cataloging-in-Publication Data

Block, Jay A.
   101 best cover letters / Jay Block, Michael Betrus.
       p. cm.
   Includes index.
   ISBN 0-07-134257-5 (pbk.)
   1. Cover letters. I. Betrus, Michael. II. Title. III. Title:
One hundred one best cover letters. IV. Title: One hundred and one
best cover letters.
HF5383.B533   1999
808'.0665—dc21
                                     99-19053
                                        CIP

McGraw-Hill

A Division of The McGraw·Hill Companies

1 2 3 4 5 6 7 8 9 0 MAL/MAL 9 0 4 3 2 1 0 9

ISBN 0-07-134257-5

McGraw-Hill books are available at special quantity discounts to use as premiums and sales promotions, or for use in corporate training sessions. For more information, please write to the Director of Special Sales, McGraw-Hill, 11 West 19th Street, New York, NY 10011. Or contact your local bookstore.

Contents

Contributors

Acknowledgments

We would like to thank all the members of PARW who collectively have raised the bar of excellence in the area of resume writing and job coaching. Their contributions have made it possible for more people around the globe to find passion and purpose in their work.

We would also like to thank Betsy Brown, our editor at McGraw-Hill, for sponsoring the "101 ..." series, and enabling our message to reach career designers everywhere.

I also want to thank my two sons, Ian and Ryco, and my wife Dada for their love and support.

JAY A. BLOCK

I would like to thank my parents and brother for their continued support, as well as my wife Dawn for her support and putting up with my long nights working on the "101 ..." series.

MICHAEL BETRUS

101 Best Cover Letters

1

How to Use This Guide

Welcome to our newest installment in the "101 ..." series, *101 Best Cover Letters*. Our first resume book, *101 Best Resumes*, has been such a huge success that we have brought you this new installment in the series, along with *More 101 Best Resumes*. These books are very benefits intensive. Many books on the market have comparable inventories of cover letters, but these, created by members of the Professional Association of Resume Writers and us, are more updated with the latest trends as well as classic layouts.

This book reviews the key structures of a successful cover letter, as well as offering a broad sampling of many different kinds of career guidance letters. We will show you over 101 different cutting-edge letters, 10 resumes that demonstrate an accomplishments-oriented approach, and special tips sections on getting that dream position.

The largest portion of the book is dedicated to showcasing the best letters that members of the Professional Association of Resume Writers have created for their clients. Every letter has been produced by a Certified Professional Resume Writer and was actually used by a client.

We have done enough research on this subject to know that most people buy a book like this for the sample letters it provides, and the instruction that accompanies them may or may not be read. So, if you choose not to read the guidelines we have set forth, please consider the following tips in using the book:

- Keep your letters focused on what you can do for employers and *their needs*. Nearly every letter received by most hiring managers focuses on how great the applicant is, but few demonstrate a clear understanding of the company's current situation.

- Don't get too stiff in your writing style. In most cases you will notice that the higher the management level, the more relaxed the writing style. Use this opportunity to show a little flair because your resume, in general, will provide you with less opportunity to show your true colors.
- Really look over the lists of suggestions throughout the book (and itemized in the Contents). They are savvy tips you won't find anywhere else.

Again, look at the many sample letters provided by the Certified Professional Resume Writers. There is a wide array of examples that should fit just about any employment related situation. You won't be able to simply copy them because they are so customized, but they will stimulate a lot of creative ideas.

The purpose of this book is to present to you an empowering philosophy to guide your job search and to assist you in writing powerfully effective letters. The philosophy is control through clarity. The letters in this book each convey a particular message. The writers are clear on what they want or what they have to offer the marketplace. You will not read a letter in this book that tells a potential employer, "Here is the story of my life. Read through my resume and if you feel I might fit in somewhere, feel free to contact me."

The letters contained in this volume will show you how to communicate with a potential employer, addressing what you can do for them, what value you bring to their organizations, why you want to contribute to their teams specifically, and what next actions you suggest to move the process forward to the next step. The purpose of this book is to provide you with examples of proactive letters so you can begin to design your own and secure the career opportunity you deserve.

SMALL DISTINCTIONS MAKE A BIG DIFFERENCE

The difference between success and failure often lies in tiny details. All things being equal, the difference between getting an interview and not getting an interview very often is the cover letter. Consider this quote from Max Messmer, Chairman and CEO of Robert Half International, Inc., the world's largest specialized staffing firm: "I would be lying if I told you that I read every resume that crossed my desk. But I have almost never not looked at a resume that was accompanied by a solid, well-written cover letter." The lesson here is: Learn how to write a strong letter. This book is intended to help you do just that.

BUT I DON'T WRITE WELL

So you don't write well, is that it? This seems to be the general consensus among job searchers and to make matters worse, most people don't like to write. Having to write a letter is bad enough, but to write a letter about ourselves can be a nearly impossible task. Well, there's only one solution to this problem: You have to change! You must learn to write a powerful letter—to communicate critical messages that will ignite enthusiasm and interest in you as a candidate.

Once you understand the importance of writing strong letters, you'll start to embrace and enjoy the art of creating your personalized messages. Here's the exciting part about the majority of letters you will be writing for securing the job you want: *You won't be focusing on yourself; rather you will be focusing on the contributions you can make and the value you bring to an organization.*

2

Uncovering New Opportunities

Before getting into the mechanics, strategy, and catalog of job search letters, we'd like to provide you with a brief overview of job search fundamentals. Entire books have been dedicated to this topic, but the most important elements are captured here. This section also appears in our resume series, and provides a concise, lean overview of job search fundamentals.

There are several primary sources of job leads:

- Networking
- Contacting companies directly
- Classified advertisements
- Executive recruiters and employment agencies
- On-line services

Other sources include trade journals, job fairs, college placement offices, and state employment offices. One of the most difficult tasks in life is securing work and planning a career. A career is important to everyone, so you must create a plan of action utilizing more than one of the career design strategies at the same time.

NETWORKING

Without question, the most common way people find out about and obtain new positions is through networking. Networking is *people connecting*, and when you connect with people you begin to assemble your network. Once your network is in place, you will continue to make new contacts and communicate with established members. People in your network will provide advice, information, and support in helping you to achieve your career goals and aspirations.

Networking accounts for up to 70 percent of the new opportunities uncovered. So what is networking? Many people assume they should call all the people they know, personally and professionally, and ask if they know of any companies that are hiring. A successful networker's approach is different.

A successful networker starts by listing as many names as possible on a sheet of paper. These can include family, relatives, friends, coworkers and managers (past and present), other industry contacts, and anyone else you know. The next step is to formulate a networking presentation. Keep in mind it need not address potential openings. In networking the aim is to call your contacts to ask for career or industry advice. The point is, you're now positioning yourself not as a desperate job hunter but as a *researcher*.

It is unrealistic to ask people for advice like this:

> *Mark, thanks for taking some time to talk with me. My company is likely to lay people off next month and I was wondering if your company had any openings or if you know of any?*

This person hasn't told Mark what he or she does, has experience in, or wants to do. Mark is likely to respond with, "No, but I'll keep you in mind should I hear of anything." What do you think the odds are that Mark will contact this person again?

A better approach is to ask for personal or industry advice and work on developing the networking web:

> *Mark, Paul Jonathan at CNA suggested I give you a call. He and I have worked together for some time, and he mentioned you work in finance and are the controller at Allied Sensors. I work in cost accounting and feel you'd likely be able to offer some good career advice. I'd really appreciate some time. Could we get together for lunch sometime in the next week or so?*

You have now asked for advice, not a job. People will be much more willing to help someone who has made them feel good about themselves or who appears to genuinely appreciate their help. This strategy can be approached in many ways. You can ask for: job search advice (including resume or cover letter advice); overall career advice (as shown above); industry advice; information about various companies, people, industries; other people or key contacts the person may know. It is important that the person you network through likes you. When someone gives you a reference, it is a reflection on that person. They will not put themselves at personal or professional risk if they aren't confident you will be a good reflection on them. Finally, send each person you speak with a thank-you letter. That courtesy will be remembered in future contacts.

25 TIPS FOR JOB SEARCHING WHILE STILL EMPLOYED

1. Do not let your current employer find out about your intent to look around. This means no loose resumes left on the copy machine, no mailing from the office, no signals that could jeopardize your current position.

2. Get organized and commit to the job search process. Without the immediate pressure to look for a job that comes from being unemployed, you may run the risk of being sporadic in your job search efforts. You must schedule time for the search and stick to it.

3. Don't feel guilty about looking around while employed. You owe it to yourself to make the most of your career, especially in today's environment of companies looking out for their own financial health.

4. Get a voice mail pager to enable yourself to return calls quickly, or a reliable answering machine at home.

5. Do not circulate your work number for new employment purposes.

6. Do not send your resume or any other correspondence on current employer stationery.

7. Take advantage of different time zones to make calls, if this applies to you. This enables you to make calls early in the morning or after work.

8. Use a nearby fax for correspondence if you don't have one at home (but not the one at work).

9. Do not use any resources of your current employer in your job search.

10. Commit to 10 to 12 hours per week for job searching, and schedule your activities for the week during the prior weekend.

11. Utilize executive recruiters and employment agencies. In some cases they will be able to significantly cut down on your leg work.

12. Target direct mail efforts on the weekends; though the success rate is lower, it requires some less time on the weekdays than other activities.

13. Make use of lunchtime during the week to schedule phone calls and interviews.

14. Network through your family and friends.

15. Use electronic means to speed up your search, including surfing the Net for job listings and company information.

16. Try to schedule interviews and other meetings before the workday (e.g., breakfast meetings) and after 5 p.m. You'll be shocked at how many employers will try to accommodate this, and they'll appreciate your work ethics.

17. Though the hit rate may not be great, you may consider identifying a direct mail company to help you directly contact many companies. They could even direct fax for you, and the rates aren't usually too high.

18. Network during off hours and through a few professional contacts, using caution and good judgment as to who should be contacted.

19. If you are concerned about your current employer finding out about your search, leave them off your resume and note that fact in your cover letter.

20. Consider using a broadcast letter in lieu of a resume (see page 69).

21. In confidence, utilize vendors, customers, and other people associated with your current position, especially if you want to remain in your industry.

22. Contact your stock broker for ideas on growing companies.

23. Create a business calling card with your name and personal contact information. Hand them out in sync with your 1 to 2 minute prepared pitch about yourself.

24. Do not speak critically of your current employer.

25. Read your newspaper from cover to cover to determine what companies are growing, not who's advertising job openings.

CONTACTING COMPANIES DIRECTLY

Aren't there one or two companies you've always been interested in working for? Ideally you may know someone who will introduce you to key contacts there or inform you of future openings. The best way to get introduced to a targeted company is to have a current employee personally introduce you or make an introductory phone call for you. You could make the introduction and refer to the employee you know. We'll get into this later, but if you don't know anyone at a targeted company, a recruiter may be a good source of contact for you, even if it involves no job order for them.

You could send an unsolicited resume, but the likelihood of this being effective is low. Most large companies receive thousands of resumes a year, and few are acted on. Corporate recruiters Jackie Larson and Cheri Comstock, authors of *The New Rules of the Job Search Game*, don't regard mass-mailed resumes very seriously. Part of the problem is that too many resumes are written as past job descriptions and are not *customized* toward a targeted position.

Conrad Lee, a Boca Raton recruiter, believes "information is the most important thing in contacting companies directly. Don't call just one person in the company and feel that is sufficient. That person may have job insecurities or be on a performance improvement plan. You should contact five to ten people and only then can you say you contacted that company directly." New job search strategies all suggest targeting a select few smaller companies (under 750 employees, as larger companies are still downsizing) intensely rather than blanketing a thousand generically. Contacting the head of your functional specialty in that company is a good start. Is it hard? Of course. You're facing rejection, probably feeling like you're bothering busy people or begging, and maybe even feeling inferior. Would you feel inferior if you were calling hotels and ticket agencies for Super Bowl information? Of course not. What if some can't help you? You just get back on the phone until you achieve your goal. These contacts should be approached in the same way. You have a great product to sell—yourself. Position yourself as someone of value and as a product that can contribute to the target company.

The key is to position yourself for individual situations. This requires specialized letters, resumes, and strategies tailored for each situation.

One trick is to call the company you are targeting and try to get the name of the person in charge of the department you would like to work in. If you don't know, call the receptionist and ask her or him who that is, and perhaps who a vendor or two might be (such as an accounting firm or ad agency). Finally, check their Web site for the latest company news. Now you have something interesting to talk about when you reach the hiring manager.

25 SALARY NEGOTIATING TIPS

1. From the moment you make initial contact with any company or organization you wish to work with, you are in negotiations. You may not be discussing money openly, but you are making a permanent imprint on the minds of the hiring authorities.

2. Delay all discussions of salary until there is an offer on the table.

3. You are in the strongest negotiating position as soon as the offer is made.

4. Know your value. You must know how you can contribute to the organization. Establish this in the mind of the hiring manager.

5. Get employers enthusiastic about your candidacy and they will become more generous.

6. There is no substitute for preparation. If you are well prepared, you'll be confident, self-assured, and poised for success.

7. Prior to going into employment negotiations, you must know the average salary paid for similar positions with other organizations in your geographical area.

8. Prior to going into employment negotiations you must know, as best you can, the salary range the company you're interviewing with will pay, or what former employees were earning.

9. Prior to going into employment negotiations you must know your personal needs and requirements, and how they relate to tips 7 and 8.

10. Remember, fringes and perks, such as vacation time, flex time, health benefits, pension plans, and so on have value. Consider the "total" salary package.

11. Salary negotiations must be win-win negotiations. If they're not, everybody loses in the end.

12. Be flexible; don't get hung up on trivial issues, and always seek compromise when possible.

13. Listen carefully and pay close attention. Your goals will most likely be different from the goals of the employer. For instance, the firm's main focus might be base salary. Yours might be total earning potential. So a win-win solution might be to negotiate a lower base salary but a higher commission or bonus structure.

14. Anticipate objections and prepare effective answers to these objections.

15. Try to understand the employer's point of view. Then plan a strategy to meet both the employer's concerns and your needs.

16. Don't be afraid to negotiate out of fear of losing the offer. Most employers *expect* you to negotiate as long as you negotiate in a fair and reasonable manner.

17. Always negotiate in a way that reflects your personality, character, and work ethic. Remain within your comfort zone.

18. Never lose control. Remain enthusiastic and upbeat even if the negotiations get a little hot. This might be your first test under fire.

19. Play hardball only if you're willing to walk away from, or lose, the deal.

20. What you lose in the negotiations will most likely never be recouped. Don't be careless in preparing for or conducting the negotiations.

21. Be sure to get the offer and final agreement in writing.

22. You should feel comfortable asking the employer for 24 to 48 hours to think about the deal if you need time to think it over.

23. Never link salary to personal needs or problems. Compensation should always be linked to your value.

24. Understand your leverage. Know whether you are in a position of strength or weakness and negotiate intelligently based on your personal situation.

25. End salary negotiations on a friendly and cheerful note.

CLASSIFIED ADVERTISING

When you depend on classified advertisements to locate job openings you limit yourself to only 7 to 10 percent or fewer of all available jobs, plus you are competing with thousands of job hunters who are reading the same ads. Keep in mind that the majority of these ads are for lower-wage positions. Do not disregard the classifieds, but at the same time don't limit your options by relying too heavily on them. Answering ads is more effective at lower levels than higher. An entry-level position or administrative support position is more likely to be found using this method than a director's position. But it is easy to review advertisements. Check the local paper listings on Sunday, the paper of the largest metropolitan area near where you live, and even a few national papers like the *Wall Street Journal* (or their advertisement summary, the *National Business Employment Weekly*) or the *New York Times*.

You may gain company insight by looking at the ads that don't necessarily match your background. You may see an ad that says, "Due to our expansion in the Northeast we are looking for ... ." You have just learned of an expanding company that may need you. Review papers that have good display ads like the *Los Angeles Times*, the *Chicago Tribune*, or any other major Sunday edition.

Tactically, here is an interesting suggestion. Use the thought process above and call the company. Many classified ads list a fax number, but no company name or main number. They encourage you to fax your resume, but not to call them. In most companies, a fax number is a derivative extension of the main number. So, if the fax number is NXX-5479, there is a good chance that the main number is NXX-5000 or NXX-5400. With that information you can call the company and hunt for information, write a more interesting and industry specific letter, and position yourself ahead of the people who didn't use this method.

When you write a cover letter, write about the company, not just "...I am answering your ad ... ." Package the resume and cover letter in a U.S. priority mail envelope so it stands out, and you will be guaranteed to at least have your resume reviewed. When answering an ad, that is your first objective.

EXECUTIVE RECRUITERS AND EMPLOYMENT AGENCIES

Employment agencies and executive recruiters work for the hiring companies, not for you. There are thousands of employment agencies and executive recruiters nationwide. Employment agencies generally place candidates in positions with a salary range under $40,000. Executive recruiters place candidates from temporary service at the administrative or executive level to permanent, senior level management. Recruiters can be a great source of hidden jobs, even if they do not have a position suitable for you at a given time.

Recruiters and agencies have a greater chance of successfully locating a position for you if your professional discipline is of a technical or specific nature, such as accounting, engineering, or sales.

25 UNCONVENTIONAL TECHNIQUES FOR UNCOVERING AND SECURING NEW OPPORTUNITIES

1. If you see a classified ad that sounds really good for you but only lists a fax number and no company name, try to figure out the company by trying similar numbers. For example, if the fax number is 555-4589, try 555-4500 or 555-4000. Get the company name and contact person so you can send a more personalized letter and resume.

2. Send your resume in a Priority Mail envelope for the serious prospects. It only costs $3 but your resume will stand out and get you noticed.

3. Check the targeted company's Web site; they may have job postings there that others without computer access haven't seen.

4. If you see a classified ad for a good prospective company but a different position, contact the company anyway. If they are new in town (or even if they're not), they may have other, non-advertised openings.

5. Always have a personalized card with you in case you meet a good networking or employment prospect.

6. Always have a quick personal briefing rehearsed in case you meet someone who could be helpful in your job search.

7. Network in non-work environments, such as a happy hour bar (a great opportunity to network) or an airport.

8. Network with your college alumni office. Many college graduates list their current employers with that office, and they may be good sources of leads, even out of state.

9. Most newspapers list all the new companies that have applied for business licenses. Check that section and contact the ones that appear appealing to you.

10. Call your attorney and accountant and ask them if they can refer you to any companies or business contacts; perhaps they have good business relationships that may be good for you to leverage.

11. Contact the Chamber of Commerce for information on new companies moving into the local area.

12. Don't give up if you've had just one rejection from a company you are targeting. You shouldn't feel you have truly contacted that company until you have contacted at least three different people there.

13. Join networking clubs and associations that will expose you to new business contacts.

14. Ask your stockbroker for tips on which companies are fast-growing and good companies to grow with.

15. Make a list of everyone you know and use them all as network sources.

16. Put an endorsement portfolio together (see page 135) and mail it out with targeted resumes.

17. Employ the hiring proposal strategy (see page 147).

18. Post your resume on the Internet, selecting news groups and bulletin boards that will readily accept it and that match your industry and discipline.

19. Don't forget to demonstrate passion and enthusiasm when you are meeting with people, interviewing with them, and networking through them.

20. Look at your industry's trade journals. Nearly all industries and disciplines have multiple journals, and most journals have an advertising section in the back that lists potential openings with companies and re-

cruiters. This is a great resource in today's low unemployment environment.

21. Visit a job fair. There won't be managerial positions recruited for but there will be many companies present, and you may discover a hot lead. If companies are recruiting in general, you should contact them directly for a possible fit.

22. Don't overlook employment agencies. They may seem like a weak possibility, but they may uncover a hidden opportunity or serve as sources to network through.

23. Look for companies that are promoting their products using a lot of advertising. Sales are probably going well and they may be good hiring targets for you.

24. Call a prospective company and simply ask who their recruiting firm is. If they have one they'll tell you, and then you can contact that firm to get in the door.

25. Contact every recruiter in town. Befriend them and use them as networking sources if possible. Always thank them, to the point of sending them a small gift for helping you out. This will pay off in dividends in the future. Recruiters are always good contacts.

25 INTERVIEWING TIPS

1. Relax. The employment interview is just a meeting. Although you should not treat this meeting lightly, don't forget that the organization interviewing you is in need of your services as much as, or perhaps more than, you are of theirs.

2. The key to successful interviewing is rapport building. Most people spend their time preparing for interviews by memorizing canned responses to anticipated questions. Successful interviewers spend most of their time practicing the art of rapport building through the use of powerfully effective communicating techniques.

3. Prepare a manila folder that you will bring to the interview. Include in the folder:
   - company information (annual reports, sales material, etc.);
   - extra resumes (6 to 12) and your letters of reference;
   - 15 questions you've prepared based on your research and analysis of the company;
   - a blank legal pad, pen, and anything else you consider helpful (e.g., college transcripts).

4. Dress appropriately. Determine the company's dress code and meet it. If their dress is business casual, you still need to be dressed in business professional. Practice proper grooming and hygiene.

5. Shoes, of course, must be polished.

6. Wear limited jewelry.

7. Call the day before to confirm the appointment—it will set you apart.

8. Be certain that you know exactly where you're going. Arrive in plenty of time. You should be at the receptionist's desk 10 to 12 minutes before the scheduled interview.

9. Prior to meeting the receptionist, check your appearance. Check your hair, clothing, and general image. Test your smile.

10. Secretaries, administrative assistants, and receptionists often have a say in the hiring process. Make a strong first impression with them.

11. Look around the office and search for artifacts that disclose the personality and culture of the company—and possibly the interviewer. This information will be helpful in initially breaking the ice, when you first begin discussions.

12. Be aware of your body language. Sit erect, with confidence. When standing and walking, move with confidence!

13. Your handshake should be firm, made with a wide-open hand, fingers stretched wide apart. Women should feel comfortable offering their hands and a firm and friendly handshake. A power handshake and great smile will get you off to a great start.

14. Eye contact is one of the most powerful forms of communicating. It demonstrates confidence, trust, and power.

15. During the interview, lean forward toward the interviewer. Show enthusiasm and sincere interest.

16. Take notes during the interview. You may want to refer to them later in the interview. If you are uncomfortable with this, ask permission first.

17. Be prepared for all questions, especially uncomfortable ones. Before the interview, script out a one-page response for each question that poses a problem for you and practice repeating it until you're comfortable with it.

18. Communicate your skills, qualifications, and credentials to the hiring manager. Describe your market value and the benefits you offer. *Demonstrate how you will contribute to the bottom line.* Show how you can 1) improve sales, 2) reduce costs, 3) improve productivity, or 4) solve organizational problems.

19. Key in on *specific accomplishments*. Accomplishments determine your hiring appeal. They separate the winners from the runners-up.

20. Listening skills are priceless! Job offers are made to those who listen well, find hidden meanings, and answer questions in a brief but effective manner.

21. Let the interviewer bring up salary first. The purpose of an interview is to determine whether there is a match. Once that is determined, salary should then be negotiated.

22. There is no substitute for planning and preparation, practice and rehearsing—*absolutely none.*

23. Practice interviewing techniques using video technology. A minimum of five hours of video practice, preferably more, guarantees a stellar performance.

24. Close the sale. If you find you want the position, ask for it. Ask directly, "Is there anything that would prevent you from offering me this position now?" or, "Do you have any reservations or concerns?" (if you sense that). At the very least, this should flush out any objections and give you the opportunity to turn them into positives.

25. Always send a thank-you note within 24 hours of every employment meeting.

3

Cover Letters as Easy as PIE

A WORKING DEFINITION OF A COVER LETTER

A cover letter is a formal communication introducing a candidate and his or her credentials (usually but not always via a resume) to a potential employer for the purpose of igniting interest in that candidate as a potential employee.

Very few people invest time and effort to composing a strong and compelling letter. Why? Because it is challenging and in many cases requires more creativity than writing a resume. When you commit to writing strong letters in pursuit of your career goals and aspirations, you will achieve a level of satisfaction only a fraction of the population will ever experience.

MAKING A GOOD FIRST IMPRESSION

Ask any job candidate why he or she takes great pains in selecting the right wardrobe when going to an interview and the answer might be, "In order to make a smashing first impression." In the majority of cases, the candidate does not get the chance to make the first impression face to face. Even the resume makes the second impression behind the cover letter. The very first impression is made by the letter that introduces the resume—the cover letter. Many cover letters are poorly written with little information to spark any interest in the writer. They are clumsily put together with little thought given to who will be reading the document.

A salesperson who puts together a proposal for a large bid will take the time and put in the effort to make it the very best proposal it can be—a proposal that will address and meet the important needs of the client. The cover letter and resume must perform the same function as the proposal.

The cover letter must address and meet the important needs of the prospective employer in a professional and entertaining fashion.

THE PIE METHOD FOR WRITING COVER LETTERS

If you want to break away from the 90 percent who follow the pack, look alike, and experience the same results, compose all your job search and career design letters with the PIE method in mind.

P = Passion

Write with enthusiasm, energy, and passion. The world is full of dull, boring, and monotonous letters that don't communicate enough and do not draw the connection between the company's needs and what the candidate can offer.

The resume is a formal document that tells the same story to all who read it. The cover letter, on the other hand, is a means for connecting with the reader and presenting yourself as an exciting human being—with a personality that accompanies your skills and qualifications. A cover letter allows you to build rapport with the reader when you write with enthusiasm. Passion helps overcome many obstacles and liabilities. Often a candidate with educational or experience related deficiencies can successfully conquer these seemingly insurmountable hurdles by writing or speaking in an impassioned and energetic way. Notice the subtle differences between the following two paragraphs:

1. I am a hardworking individual recognized for increasing sales on a consistent basis. I have over 20 years of successful experience in computer sales and work well in high stress or pressure arenas.

Or...

2. IBM is in a transition of moving to more value-added services that require a more consultative sales approach. I have a consistent, verifiable record of selling very customized business solutions packages that require a clear understanding of the customer's needs, spanning 20 years in fast-track environments.

Be sure when you write that what you write is said with a degree of passion, excitement, and emotion. Right or wrong, fair or unfair, a lifeless letter reflects a lifeless person.

I = Interest

Using passionate words but having little to say is a waste of passion. Obviously you must have something of interest to say that will result in a prospective employer developing a strong interest in you as a potential contributor to the organization. You must determine, in advance of writing the letter, what information will spark interest. You may want to visit *101 Best Resumes* (McGraw-Hill, 1999), Chapter 3, "Taking Inventory of Your Skills," for a comprehensive guide to identifying your skills for both your resume and cover letter.

Your most important job of all, prior to writing a letter of any kind, is to investigate, research, and uncover the critical messages you feel must be conveyed to generate immediate interest in you. The first two guidelines for writing powerfully effective cover letters are to have something of interest to communicate to the reader and to deliver that message with passion and enthusiasm.

Another equally important way to generate interest is to address the company's needs as you understand them and draw the connection between those needs and your skills as means to meet them. You must determine the company or hiring manager's "hot buttons." For example, if you are a marketing manager in the telecommunications industry applying for a position with Sprint PCS, mention that you understand the company's needs:

> *Mr. Robinson, Sprint PCS is in an aggressive start-up mode, and you will need people who have a working knowledge of the skills it takes to successfully manage a start-up. I know that includes setting up new distribution channels and new retailers, working with the RF engineers on prioritizing the network build-out and developing aggressive but fiscally responsible pricing strategies. Over the past five years, I have been … .*

E = Excellence

A potential employer wants to know your level of commitment to excellence. Today's market is a shrinking, global village where only the fittest will survive. Most companies are following in the footsteps of the U.S. Marines—they are looking for a few good people. The competition is stiff for the few good jobs. Langberg, McHugh and Company, a marketing consulting firm, performed a research study of high-level functional managers and what their top business needs were. Two of the top five were hiring good people and retaining good people.

Though it may seem difficult to find a position, hiring managers in today's economy suggest it is just as difficult to find good hires. You need to be able to package yourself for that first dynamic introduction so you will be perceived as a "good hire."

In order for you to be considered a possible candidate, your commitment to excellence must show through in the cover letter. You must communicate the level of integrity, confidence, competence, and trustworthiness that top employers seek. In the end, a powerful cover letter embodies a compelling message, depicts a professional commitment to excellence in one's chosen discipline, and is communicated with passion and emotion.

ONE RULE ONLY

There can be no spelling, typographical, or grammatical errors on the document. It must be well-organized and professionally presented consistently with the industry or organization you are approaching.

JOB SEARCHING IS ACTUALLY SALES AND MARKETING

The concept of career design is analogous to marketing and sales. First, as in market research, you must identify your target customer, or company. Then you must decide how to position yourself, what your overall message is (keep this narrow, as in advertising), and how to develop the marketing materials to communicate the message (your cover letter and resume). The sales process is actually the phone follow-up and the interview process.

Have you noticed how creative some companies' advertising campaigns have become? Pepsi is using flying geese, Microsoft used the Rolling Stones to reach a different market, and Nike is using its sports proteges in all kinds of creative advertisements. Make no mistake, in today's economy the great positions are out there. You just need to have the right product (your skill set) and the right packaging (your cover letter and resume) to get in the door.

4

Cover Letters and the Ten Commandments

COMMANDMENT 1
DEVELOP A MASTER TEAM OF ADVISORS TO HELP YOU WRITE AND EDIT THE LETTERS

One common thread that seems to connect successful people is that they consistently surround themselves with other successful people. The purpose of developing an effective Master Team of Advisors (two to five people) is to surround yourself with key people who will become your guardian angels, support group, and sounding board, not only in drafting powerful letters but in the entire job search and career design process. They will guide you when you steer off track, they will catch you up when you fall, and they will celebrate when you achieve victory.

Your Master Team of Advisors can be made up of friends, family members, teachers, former supervisors—anyone who brings strength, confidence, and career management expertise to the process. Obviously each member must be able to contribute, and you'll need to select at least one to two members who have outstanding communication skills, both verbal and written. Your Master Team will help ensure that your letters are crisp, full of emotion, and on the message.

COMMANDMENT 2
PERSONALIZE AND CUSTOMIZE EACH LETTER

Whenever possible address your letter to a specific person. People like to hear their names in conversation and see their names in print. By identifying a person by name and title you show respect and an added degree of professionalism. You want to give every indication that this is a personalized marketing letter, not a form letter.

Recall the discussion in Chapter 3 about the importance of drawing the connection between the company's needs and your skills. There is very little difference between marketing a new product and marketing yourself for a new position. You must personalize each letter and resume to score a direct hit on the prospective employer's hot buttons.

COMMANDMENT 3
WRITE WITH THE READER IN MIND

The main objective of a cover letter is to get an interview or to take the hiring process to the next step. You will get the interview or advance to the next step if you meet the prospective company's "criteria for hire." Your job is to determine what those criteria are and demonstrate that you meet them. Place yourself in the hiring manager's shoes and ask yourself, "What would I want if I were hiring a person for this position?" Your letter must address and answer the following questions:

- What is the company really looking for? What do they need?
- What qualifications do I have that are valuable to a potential employer?
- What specific contributions have I made in the past that will excite this employer?
- What type of personality do I have and am I a team player?
- Why do I want to work for this company?
- What separates me from the rest of the field?

COMMANDMENT 4
THE LETTER MUST BUILD RAPPORT WITH THE READER

People generally hire people they like or who are like them. One of the most understated objectives of any letter, especially a cover letter, is to build rapport with the reader. Writing is an art—we can make people laugh and cry just by the words we choose. We can get people excited or turn them off by the vocabulary we incorporate in our letters, so select your words carefully. Be sure there is an air of warmth and sentiment in your writing. Most people do not take the time to write with emotion. If you do, you will give yourself a solid advantage in the quest for the right job opportunity.

COMMANDMENT 5
SEDUCE THE READER—PROVIDE A REASON TO ACT

An employer receives 100 resumes and decides to interview 8 candidates. Question: What did the employer see in the 8 resumes that he or she didn't see in the other 92?

You job is to give this question serious thought *before* you put the letter together. Those who distinguish themselves from the rest of the competition are those who get hired. Your job is to match your skills and qualifications with a prospective employer's needs. Once you determine what those critical needs are, you can show employers what they want to see. Seducing the reader means communicating in a letter that which the reader wants to see. When you are able to do that, the reader will take action—calling you in for an interview!

COMMANDMENT 6
DON'T REHASH YOUR RESUME

Cover letters need to enhance and support the resume, *not* repeat what is already on it. Your job is to find different ways to reinforce the critical messages to entice the reader to want to meet with you. Be original and refreshing and be careful not to repeat what you already wrote in your resume.

Have you ever created a PowerPoint presentation and had to deliver it to an internal audience or to a customer? Have you ever used the notes' sections at the bottom of a slide as a prompt for discussion points? Imagine that your resume is the presentation and that the notes or talking points are your cover letter. Your cover letter should embellish and interpret your resume in a manner that the reader will be receptive to.

COMMANDMENT 7
SHORTER IS BETTER

Don't ramble! Most employment professionals spend less than 30 seconds reviewing both the cover letter and the resume. The lesson here is simple: Be sharp, be brief, and be powerful in your choice of words. Get to the point and unless you have a very good reason to do otherwise, keep the letter to one page in length.

COMMANDMENT 8
SEEKING PROFESSIONAL ASSISTANCE MAY BE A GOOD IDEA

What do Ford, General Electric, Microsoft, Nabisco, and probably every other Fortune 1000 company have in common? They hire advertising and marketing professionals to help promote their products and services because they are *too close* to the subject matter and cannot write objectively. The same holds true for you. When a company creates a product, the product developers become very proud of all the great things the product can do. They want to communicate 20 messages at once to the customers as to why their product is best.

Professional marketers and advertisers understand that you cannot send mixed or complex messages to prospective customers. You get to highlight one or maybe two messages. Marketers identify who the target base of customers is (like your base of targeted employers) and what the customers' needs are (as you identify the needs of the prospective employer). They then craft a crisp message drawing the connection between the customers' needs and the product's features and benefits.

Many professional marketers and copy writers are very skilled at writing a boiled-down positioning statement or advertising message. If you either are in a rut or have a big opportunity coming up, consider utilizing a professional to help you write your letters or your resume. This can get a little pricey, especially if you're out of work, but with the payoff of a new position and higher salary, it can be a good investment.

Caution: It is your responsibility to be an active participant in the letter writing process even if you hire a writing professional. Be sure the words and concepts you use can be defended. Be sure the writing style matches your speaking style. Don't use words you wouldn't use or ideas you cannot comfortably defend. The bottom line is this: The letter must be congruent with you. If the letter is high-powered and highly energetic but you are a low-key, quiet type, when you finally get to the interview it will be obvious to the interviewer that you did not write the letter. Seeking out professional help is fine so long as you work as a team to express what you are comfortable expressing.

COMMANDMENT 9
BE DIFFERENT AND DISTINCTIVE, BUT DON'T GET CUTE

There's a difference between creative writing and foolish or inappropriate writing. Obviously you do not have to open your letter with a boring or conventional standard sentence, but don't go so far as to open it with a turn-off. Know your market, know the people who will be reading the letters, and know how far you can go. This differs from industry to industry and even manager to manager. On top of that, even if you send your letter to one manager, it is likely that many will see it as you make the rounds to interview. A strong, creative, and high-impact opening will go a long way in getting you noticed. An attention-grabber that is offensive or just plain silly will go a long way in hurting any chances you have of being considered for the position.

COMMANDMENT 10
THE LETTER MUST REFLECT PROFESSIONALISM

The letter must be highly professional, from the paper stock to how it's delivered. The letter must be grammatically perfect with no typographical or spelling errors. It is common knowledge that most hiring managers believe that the professionalism a candidate represents in the job search process will be the same degree of professionalism he or she will bring to the job. There is a big difference between folding your resume and cover letter into thirds and mailing them in a plain #10 envelope, and sending them Federal Express or U.S. Priority Mail. Do not ever underestimate the importance of class, style, and professionalism!

5
Anatomy of a Cover Letter

I. HEADING

(Include name, address, phone number, fax number, E-mail address, etc.)

Patrick D. Dudash
1801 West Cortney Street
West Palm Beach, FL 33409
Phone: (561) 555-1234 / Fax: (561) 555-4321
Pdudash@scapenet.net

The heading does not have to include all of the items listed here. Name, address, and telephone are critical, but fax number and E-mail address are optional. If you include your E-mail address, make sure you check it often. If you list a fax number, make sure you check it as well. Of all things, do not use your current employer's fax number or E-mail address unless you have prior approval.

II. DATE

September 5, 1998

III. NAME, TITLE, COMPANY NAME, AND ADDRESS OF RECIPIENT

Ms. Maria Lane, Executive Vice President
Hyde and Smithson Public Relations, Inc.
1800 Scenic Way
Mountain View, VT 19877

The critical point here is to make sure you include the company name and the recipient's title, if you know it.

IV. SALUTATION

Dear Ms. Lane:

V. POWER INTRODUCTION

(Attention-grabber, generating interest and stating why you want to work for this employer.)

Over the last few months I've noticed your firm moving into consulting with several health care firms. After speaking with Mike Kiryn, I am aware that you are bidding on the upcoming opening of two new Columbia hospitals. You will no doubt need significant health care industry expertise to drive this account. Health care can really get complicated when trying to balance aggressive marketing and sales techniques along with a caring public entity image.

I have been working in marketing and public relations for 9 years, most recently with Humana in Florida. We successfully opened 11 new hospitals over the last 6 years, and even experienced a storm when we opened the one in Orlando. That one opened in the midst of a major citywide controversy about the rising cost of health care and much criticism was directed our way in the media. Under my direction Humana successfully overcame that encounter and now that hospital is one of the most successful in the region.

Notice that the letter opens by giving Ms. Lane an understanding that the applicant knows the business, and then ties her needs into Mr. Dudash's background.

VI. PURPOSE OF THE LETTER

After working with Humana for several years, I feel I need a change. I have informed our regional director that I will be relocating to the Northeast and would like to move into the consulting arena, supporting the health care industry. After 15 years in the industry in key public relations roles, and after seeing the explosion in the industry with too many green managers making fundamental mistakes, I know I can offer a wealth of knowledge to improve their operations. I have many key contacts in the industry but am not interested in starting up a consulting operation of my own. I can provide a solid lead list to broaden your client list.

VII. CRITICAL MESSAGES

I offer your consulting service the following skills:
- *15 years in public relations*
- *15 years in the health care industry*
- *Expertise in new launches and crisis management*
- *Key contacts within the industry*

VIII. CALL TO ACTION

You must initiate the next step.

Please expect my telephone call in the next week so that we can set a time to meet and discuss employment possibilities that would serve our mutual interests.

IX. CLOSE

Thanks for your consideration. I look forward to meeting with you soon.
Sincerely,
Patrick Dudash

As with any letter, you can use block-style paragraph format (shown here) or indent the first line. Both are equally acceptable, though the block style is used more often in business.

Though this letter would be two pages long, it does a comprehensive job of illustrating the connection between the applicant's skills and the company's needs. A longer letter is permissible for a higher-level, highly targeted letter like this.

25 TIPS FOR WRITING COVER LETTERS

1. Use customized stationery with your name, address, and phone number on top. Match your stationery to that of your resume—it shows class and professionalism.
2. Customize the cover letter. Address it to a specific individual. Be sure you have the proper spelling of the person's name, his or her title, and the company name.
3. If you don't wish to customize each letter and prefer to use a form letter, use the salutation "Dear Hiring Manager." (Do not use "Dear Sir." The hiring manager may be a woman.)
4. The cover letter is more informal than the resume and must begin to build rapport. Be enthusiastic, energetic, and motivating.
5. The cover letter must introduce you and your value to a potential employer.
6. Be sure to date the cover letter.
7. An effective cover letter should be easy to read, have larger typeface than the resume (12 point type is a good size), and be kept short—4 to 5 short paragraphs will usually do the job.

8. Keep the cover letter to one page. If you are compelled to use two pages, be sure your name appears on the second page.

9. The first paragraph should ignite interest in your candidacy and spark enthusiasm from the reader. Why is the reader reading this letter? What can you do for him or her?

10. The second paragraph must promote your value. What are your skills, abilities, qualifications, and credentials that would meet the reader's needs and job requirements?

11. The third paragraph notes specific accomplishments, achievements, and educational experience that would expressly support the second paragraph. Quantify these accomplishments if possible.

12. The fourth paragraph must generate future action. Ask for an interview or tell the reader that you will be calling in a week or so to follow up.

13. The fifth paragraph should be a short one, closing the letter and showing appreciation.

14. Demonstrate specific problem-solving skills in the letter, supported by specific examples.

15. Unless asked to do so, don't discuss salary in a cover letter.

16. If salary history or requirements are asked for, provide a modest window (low to mid thirties, for example) and mention that salary is negotiable (if it is).

17. Be sure the letter has a professional appearance.

18. Be sure there are no spelling, typographical, or grammatical errors.

19. Be sure to keep the letter short and to the point. Don't ramble on and on.

20. Do not lie or exaggerate. Everything you say in a cover letter and resume must be supported in the eventual interview.

21. Be careful not to use the pronoun *I* excessively. Tie together what the company is doing and what their needs might be. To come full circle, explain how you fit into their strategy and can close potential gaps in meeting their objectives.

22. Avoid negative and controversial subject matter. The purpose of a cover letter and resume is to put your best foot forward. This material (job hopping, prior termination, etc.) can be tactfully addressed in the interview.

23. If you are faxing the cover letter and resume, you need not send a fax transmittal form as long as your fax number is included in the heading along with your telephone number.

24. To close the letter, use *Sincerely, Sincerely yours, Respectfully,* or *Very truly yours.*

25. Be sure to sign the letter.

6

Targeted Cover Letters Aimed at Specific Companies

Targeted cover letters are the most effective cover letters. A targeted cover letter is written to a specific company and specific manager, for a specific position, with a specific message in mind. Because they are so specific, their success rate is higher than for a generic letter and resume mailed in bulk.

KNOW YOUR SKILLS

With a targeted letter, the first step is to identify your skills and marketable attributes. There are three categories of skills to review:

- Job-related skills
- Transferable skills
- Self-management skills

JOB-RELATED SKILLS

There are four categories of job-related skills: 1) working with people, 2) working with data and information, 3) working with things, and 4) working with ideas. Though most of us work with all four categories at one time or another, we tend to be attracted to one or two areas in particular. Successful teachers, customer service representatives, and salespeople must be particularly skilled at working with people. Financial controllers, meteorologists, and statistical forecasters possess outstanding skills in working with data and information. Engineers, mechanics, and computer technicians enjoy using their skills to work with things; and inventors, writers, and advertising professionals must have solid creativity and idea skills.

Which category do you tend toward? *Determine which job-related skills you are strongest in and which you enjoy the most. Then write a brief paragraph stating why you feel you are skilled and qualified to work in the category you selected.*

TRANSFERABLE SKILLS

Transferable skills are just that—transferable from one environment to another. If you enjoy working with people, your specific transferable skills might include leadership, training, entertainment, mentoring, mediation, persuasion, public speaking, conflict resolution, or problem-solving skills. If you enjoy working with data and information, your specific transferable skills might include research, analysis, proofreading, editing, arranging, budgeting, assessing, measuring, evaluating, surveying, or pricing. If you enjoy working with things, your specific transferable skills might include knowledge of equipment, repair, maintenance, installation, set-up, troubleshooting, or building. Finally, if you enjoy working with ideas, your specific transferable skills might include creating, developing, reengineering, restructuring, painting, writing, problem solving, planning, or brainstorming.

So take fifteen minutes, sit down with a pen and paper, and write down all the skills and abilities you possess *that have value to another company.* Transferable skills are marketable and tangible qualifications that will have value to many organizations. An accountant, human resources manager, or logistics manager at General Motors has tangible transferable skills that are of value to many companies both in and out of the automotive industry.

SELF-MANAGEMENT SKILLS

Self-management skills are skills that are personality and value oriented. Self-management skills are those that describe your attitude and work ethic. They include creativity, energy, enthusiasm, logic, resourcefulness, productive competence, persistence, adaptability, and self-confidence. One cautionary note, however: *Try not to be too general in describing your self-management skills*. When you identify a specific skill, always be prepared to explain how that skill will benefit a prospective employer. For example, if you're analytical, how does that make you better prepared for a position you have designed for yourself?

TARGETING

The next step is to target the company. You have identified your skill set and should by now have ideas on what industry you want work in. The next step is to identify which companies you want to work for. You will have some ideas off the top of your head and can identify others by several parameters. Narrow the company list down by geographic level (region or city), by industry, and by products.

Once you identify some prospective companies, you need to find out what they are looking for. What is their trend over the last one or two years, and what are their strategic plans for the next few years? How do or can your skills line up with their strategic objectives? Those are the things you will need to find out in order to target your letter and overall presentation effectively. How can you find this out? Try to network through other employees, look in the paper for recent news, check out their Web site, and do a search on the Web for more news. Best of all, call the company directly and ask them.

6-1

PETER J. MARQUARD, A.I.A.
931 South Mission Road, Suite B, Fallbrook, California 92028 • 555-1212

January 7, 1998

Mr. Larry Orlando
ABCD Corporation
123 Some Street
Fallbrook, California 92028

> *Excellent use of opening letter by mentioning common acquaintance to keep reader's attention.*

Dear Mr. Orlando:

I am writing at the recommendation of our mutual acquaintance, John Jones, who suggested I contact you concerning job opportunities as an Architect. Please accept this letter and accompanying résumé as evidence of my interest in applying for such a position with your company.

My enclosed résumé clearly shows I have a variety of qualifying skills and abilities compatible with positions as an Architect. Briefly, they are:

- Considerable experience in the field of construction and architecture augmented by a formal education and refined by specialized, industry-related training,

- A proven record of success achieved through diligence, hard work, attention to detail, and my belief in a consistent application of the fundamentals, and

- A sincere desire to contribute to the continued growth and success of your company.

After you have the opportunity to review my résumé I would like to meet with you to discuss how effectively I can contribute. I will call in a few days to arrange a meeting. Should you have any questions before scheduling an appointment, I may be reached through the number listed above.

Thank you very much for taking the time to review my résumé and for your kind consideration. I look forward to speaking with you in the near future.

Sincerely,

Peter J. Marquard

Enclosure

Robert C. Hensley
000 Bond Street • Anytown, Tennessee 37000
(615) 555-3273, cell: (615) 555-5248

July 22, 1998

Gary Hodge, Senior Vice President
S Technologies, Inc.
Civil Division
000 First Street
Suite 2
Bigcity, TN 30000

Dear Mr. Hodge:

As I enter my final semester here at Vanderbilt University in pursuit of my Master of Civil Engineering, I am exploring possible options for employment after graduation. My ideas of design and my depth of experience are not the norm for graduate students and set me above the rest of the crowd. In interest of working with S Technologies, Inc., I am enclosing my résumé for your consideration.

My background working for BSW Associates as an Engineering Technician (EIT) on large construction projects coupled with my formal education makes me an excellent candidate for employment with S Technologies, Inc. At BSW, I have been afforded the opportunity to serve as Client Manager to the town of Greensboro, Kentucky in connection with the construction of the $55 million Greensboro Bridge project. BSW was fortunate to win the bid for the bridge project after I established a working relationship with the city government of Greensboro during the recent flooding disaster the city experienced.

Greensboro is an excellent example of my skills in client acquisition and is just one of many civil accounts that I have attained for BSW. I have been able to land a total of 14 new accounts within the last two years bringing combined billings into the firm of over $96 million. I am confident I could do the same for S Technologies, Inc.

I am familiar with S Technologies, Inc. and its vast array of projects including the design and construction of the new Bigcity Arena, the suspension bridge over the Cumberland, and the water system overhaul for the metropolitan government. Most of S Technologies' major projects are government-sponsored; working with city and county governments, federal authorities, and other official entities is one of my specialties. I am comfortable working within the tangle of government red tape.

S Technologies employs professionals who are outstanding graduates, who are fast-tracking for the attainment of their PE designation, and who have innovative yet solid concepts of engineering design and client management. My record with BSW and my academic achievements speak loudly that I would make an excellent addition to your team.

I look forward to discussing this experience with you and how I can apply my client acquisition skills to benefit S Technologies. My cell phone (listed above) is probably the best means of contacting me since I am on the job site most of the day. Thank you for your consideration.

Best regards,

Robert C. Hensley

Deborah Ann Carter   3807 Deep Cavern Road • Columbus, Ohio 43127 • (614) 555-8100

> *Another good use of opening with common acquaintances to keep reader's attention.*

August 14, 1998

Dr. Martin Houser
APEC Dental Associates
432 Wildberry Lane
Columbus, Ohio 43124

Dear Dr. Houser:

Your employee, Mary Broderick, and I were in the same graduating class at Rets Technical Center, where we earned certificates in dental hygiene. Over the years, Mary and I have remained friends; and, it is at her suggestion that I am contacting you about the dental hygienist position available with APEC Dental Associates.

For the last 15 years, I have worked with Dr. Baker, who recently announced his retirement. Since Mary has always spoken so highly of your organization, I was excited to learn you have a vacancy in my career field.

As you may know, Dr. Baker has one of the busiest practices in Columbus. Therefore, I am accustomed to managing a very heavy flow of clients and maintaining an aggressive schedule.

The enclosed résumé highlights professional achievements and academic accomplishments. After reviewing it, I hope you will contact me for a personal interview.

Thank you for your time and consideration.

Sincerely,

Deborah Ann Carter

Enclosure

Leslie M. Newmann

19 Wang Court
Fairfax, CT 06999
203-555-6988
E-mail: Lmn1998@xyz.net

August 17, 1998

Mr. John Smyth
Assistant Editor
ABC Publishers, Inc.
123 Main Street
New York, NY 10000

> *Here is a good example of mother reentering the workforce, and how she made use of former and hobby-oriented accomplishments in the publishing field to meet the needs of the employer.*

Dear Mr. Smyth:

Thank you ever so much for your time on the phone this morning, and for your offer of continued help in my search for an opening on the editorial side of the publishing industry. I appreciate both your candor and your enthusiasm concerning careers in the publishing world.

As you learned in our conversation, I am now a "graduate" Mom; my three children have finished school, grown up and gone out on their own. I am more than ready to use my antique Bachelor's degree in English (1973) to serve the publishing world.

Never having held a paid position since the birth of my first child, I can't brag that I have vast previous professional experience. I have, however, sharpened my writing and editing skills on a continuing basis:

- For years, I edited high school and college essays and term papers for my children, and tutored them in English composition.
- I served as editor of our church's 100th-anniversary *Book of Memories*, an 80-page written and pictorial synopsis of parish history.
- I edited a fascinating 120-page biography written about a woman, now 95 years old, who immigrated to the United States at the turn of the century.
- I assisted in editing an article subsequently accepted for publication in a prominent pscyhology journal.

I am an avid reader, and my personal library ranges from *Red Storm Rising* to *The Language Instinct*, with supplemental periodicals including *National Geographic, Popular Science* and *Focus on the Family*. I think I could offer the right company a fine blend of diversified knowledge, a love of research and learning, a strong background in English grammar and composition and substantive computer literacy.

My questions to you are these: Where would a person with my talents, credentials and background fit in a publishing house? What door would you suggest I attempt first to open? Is there additional course work I need to pursue to make me initially eligible for editorial jobs in publishing? And is there anyone to whom you might refer me, either for further information-gathering or for potential employment?

Thank you again for the consideration you have given me. I appreciate all your assistance, and will let you know how my search progresses.

Gratefully,

ALICIA PARAMO
Route 7, Box 1776
Lakeland, Florida 33809
(555) 555-1212

August 18, 1998

> *Alicia explains her qualifications based on accomplishments to meet the needs of the employer.*

James E. Whitstone
Senior Controller
Hamilton Company
Post Office Drawer 1245
Chapel Hill, NC 27851

Dear Mr. Whitstone:

After contributing to the growth and success of USA Financial Services for 15+ years, I am seeking new challenges with an enterprising company in need of someone with exceptional planning, leadership, and analytical qualities. One of your colleagues, Bill Stephens, and I met for lunch earlier this week, and Bill recommended that I contact you regarding prospective opportunities in your department.

As evidenced in the enclosed résumé, my experience encompasses all aspects of corporate business development and operations, strategic planning, budget administration, systems integration, internal management consulting, resource utilization, and project management. My ability to analyze needs and develop unique programs designed to yield a profitable outcome has proven to be one of my greatest assets.

Credited with significantly impacting bottom-line profitability and reducing operational costs at USA Financial, I excel at modeling complex situations in order to generate investment/costing details for new business ventures. I am technologically proficient, with direct experience in remittance, imaging, and systems design and development. My record of achievements is exemplary, as I have successfully directed and managed complex assignments while meeting or exceeding anticipated scheduling and budgetary projections.

Characterized by others as visionary and decisive, I possess keen instincts and offer strategies to quickly effect change and improvement. I am equally at ease working as a team member or independently, and enjoy a leadership role where I can foster motivational and mentoring relationships with colleagues and subordinates.

I am most interested in an opportunity where I can provide strong corporate leadership and vision. I would welcome the chance to discuss with you personally the value I offer Hamilton Company. If you feel such a discussion would be beneficial, please contact me at (555) 555-1212.

Sincerely,

Alicia Paramo

Dawn M. Pitera

433 Campton, Bloomfield Hills, Michigan 48302 • (313) 555-3412 • Cell: (313) 555-3322

> *This letter is simple and not too long, but conveys enough information about Dawn's accomplishments to interest the company.*

July 20, 1997

Mr. W. J. Glencoe
Chief Executive Officer
Kendrickton Steel
123 E. Industrial Park Blvd.
Romulus, MI 48174

Dear Mr. Glencoe:

If your company is seeking a Human Resources Director who understands the relationship between employee relations and profits, then we have a good reason to talk. I have an extensive background in manufacturing, with both union and non-union workforces.

Since Human Resources represent the biggest costs to the company, these resources should also have the biggest value. With this philosophy, I have been able to implement proactive HR policies that have had a positive impact on the bottom line. As Human Resources Director for a Fortune 500 manufacturer, I have introduced financial incentives that improved productivity, reduced absenteeism, and resulted in a 15% increase in gross profits. Other accomplishments are described in my résumé.

Although I am far more interested in challenge and growth potential than salary, in recent years my total compensation has been in the $100-120K range. Salary is, of course, negotiable.

I am confident that I can help contribute to your company's bottom line. I will call you soon to see if we might schedule a meeting to learn more about one another. Thank you for your time and consideration, and I look forward to our conversation.

Sincerely,

Dawn M. Pitera
Enclosure

Mary Beth Rouse
134 Blue Moon Street
St. Joseph, Missouri 61000
(618) 555-3336

August 8, 1998

Patricia Schmidt, ASID
Patricia Schmidt Interiors
118 Frontage Drive
Fairview Heights, Illinois 62208

This targeted letter is a good example because it demonstrates the use of accomplishments in a bulleted format like a resume, but allows the writer to better articulate her story than a resume would.

Dear Ms. Schmidt:

Your name has come up in several conversations recently. As a newcomer to the area, I have been asking people if they know of any interior design companies with excellent clients and an outstanding reputation. Since I won't settle for less, perhaps you could give me fifteen minutes of your time to discuss what I have to offer.

My experience includes team design and floor plan projects for both residential and commercial buildings. I spent the last three years with Landry Bower Interiors in Kansas City, one of the most prestigious design firms in the Midwest. Among the award-winning projects I was a part of, I was most proud of these two:

- The Metropolitan Life Building renovation, a 148,000 sq. ft. high-rise office complex that challenged my knowledge of decorative styles and space planning techniques.

- The J.J. Cale Business Complex, a campus-style collection of upscale businesses with diverse themes for each building, ranging from 16th-19th century English to 19th-20th century European and American.

Although you have probably seen these buildings featured in last month's <u>Design</u> Magazine, I have enclosed a few photographs of these as well as a few of my most recent residential projects. The rest of my portfolio is available for your review.

With the possibility of landing the Union Station and St. Clair Square accounts, you should probably review the enclosed résumé giving special notice to my expertise with these types of projects in and around the Kansas City area. My guess is that once we meet, we'll know very quickly whether my skills and personality fit the needs of your company.

I will plan on picking you up for lunch next Friday afternoon unless I hear otherwise from you. Until then, please feel free to call with any questions.

Sincerely,

Mary Beth Rouse

enc.

Don Hope
11 Belexes Estates
Belleville, Illinois 62221
(618) 555-3330

Very unique letter in that it completely captures the theme of the legal profession. Excellent creativity.

	)
	) No. 12-3-456789-1
	)
Hope	)
	)
vs.	) EMPLOYMENT
	)
Reputable Law Firm	) Ed Whitney, Partner
	)
	) Hastings, Whitney, & Lowe

WHEREAS This summer my goal is to increase my exposure to the practice of law through a clerkship with a reputable law firm. The attached résumé will briefly summarize my background.

WHEREAS I can offer energy, enthusiasm, solid research skills, and strong writing abilities. Perhaps most importantly, I recognize that the seemingly endless errands assigned to a novice law clerk are an excellent foundation for understanding the day-to-day activities of an attorney, and with this understanding I am willing and even eager to take on mundane and routine tasks.

WHEREAS I am confident that my skills and energy can contribute to the smooth running of your practice. May we discuss this possibility in more detail? I will follow up with a phone call to your office the week of August 15.

Thank you for your consideration.

Sincerely,

Don Hope

Page 1

> *Letter is not too long and quickly highlights the candidate's skills and position sought.*

Patrick D. Dudash
3333 West Washington Road
Staten Island, NY 10312
508-555-4444
E-mail: JJJ4444@not.com

August 13, 1998

Mr. William Baker, Esq.
Partner
Adams, Baker & Chase, P.C.
123 Main Street
New York, NY 10000

RE: **Legal Assistant Internship**

Dear Attorney Baker:

Having graduated recently from the Legal Assistant academic program at Community College, I am now a Certified Legal Assistant. Eager to use my new skills, I have been conducting job-related research at the Career Center on campus, and there I found a posting by your firm, offering an internship opportunity for a Legal Assistant. Please accept the enclosed résumé in application for this position.

My background, although diverse, is centered in research and analysis. As a work-study student at school, I assisted the research librarian at the college library. During prior experience as a secretary, I composed correspondence, researched and compiled client files and analyzed information for the use of my employer. I look forward to the opportunity to put these skills and my newly-earned certification to use for you.

I know that my education, skills and professionalism will benefit Adams, Baker & Chase, P.C., and I believe I will be equally rewarded by the training I will receive in your law office. Thank you for your time and consideration of my qualifications; I look forward to a favorable response from you in the very near future.

Respectfully,

Patrick Dudash

Enclosure

MARIA LANE

4165 Charter Drive • Dayton, Ohio 45419 • (937) 555-1892

> *This letter is simple, direct, and will keep the interest of the reader.*

Mr. Helmut Royer
Modern Technologies Corporation
5173 East Third Street
Kettering, Ohio 45429

Excellent experience in programming and network development provide an exceptional background in creating and maintaining sophisticated information-management systems.

As a member of the MIS team of a major corporation for over eight years, I have been instrumental in creating advanced computer systems that cross industry boundaries. Prior experience includes an exemplary military career, where I was involved in planning and managing highly-complex communication projects to support worldwide operations.

As a dynamic, creative and results-driven technology professional, I am confidentially exploring opportunities that provide continuing challenge and professional growth. Therefore, the enclosed résumé is presented for your review and consideration.

I would welcome the opportunity to personally discuss my qualifications with you, and will be available at your convenience.

Thank you for your time and interest. I look forward to hearing from you soon.

Sincerely,

Maria Lane

Enclosure

GILLIAN BARR 669 Elmer Avenue • Dayton, Ohio 45402 • (937) 555-6673

August 10, 1998

Aggressive opening, this type of approach works best in positions accountable for quantitative accomplishments like sales or marketing.

Mr. John W. Rogers
Marketing Director
Jasper Paper Corporation
1410 O'Brien Street
Dayton, Ohio 45403

Dear Mr. Rogers:

Lead, follow, or get out of the way. Believing in this simple yet powerful creed has spurred me to maintain a 4.0 GPA while pursuing a bachelor's degree in business marketing. As a Fortune 100 company, Jasper Paper Corporation epitomizes the value of taking a leadership position. That's why it is my first choice for internship opportunities in marketing.

Based on academic standing, last summer I was selected to participate in a European exchange program. This experience not only broadened my cultural knowledge, but also increased awareness of the global marketplace in which today's businesses must operate.

Other degree-enhancement activities include summer employment in the Marketing Research department of NCR, and assisting the University of Dayton with launching a new adult degree program.

The possibility of working with you and your staff is exciting, and I hope you will consider me for this excellent learning experience.

Thank you for your time and interest. I will call you Friday morning, August 19th, to schedule a personal discussion, if you deem it appropriate.

Sincerely,

Gillian Barr

Enclosure

FRANK THOMPSON JR.
118 Hillside Drive, Olympia, WA 00879, (530) 555-5699

August 18, 1999

Stephanie Brown, B.S.N.
Director of Nursing
Seacouver Regional Medical Center
123 Main Street, South
Seacouver, WA 00891

> *This letter opens with a common interest of their previous meeting, a perfect introduction. The letter is also casual and very upbeat, demonstrating high energy.*

Dear Ms. Brown:

You and I had the opportunity to meet at a regional pediatrics conference eight months ago at the Hyatt Regency in downtown Olympia. During one of the lunch breaks, we discussed your efforts to expand the neonatal unit in Seacouver. I was excited to read of your success in securing the federal grant for which you worked so hard—congratulations!

The timing of your advertisement last week for a NICU Team Leader couldn't be better, as my family and I will be relocating to Seacouver next month. With over 10 years' experience as a NICU specialist at Olympia General Hospital, I believe my qualifications and experience align well with those you are seeking in the Team Leader position. Over the last several years, I have served as weekend shift supervisor in a 15-bed Level II NICU with full responsibility for patient care, team development, and budget management.

When I came onboard, there were numerous organizational challenges to be tackled. Most prevalent among them was the need to address declining morale and dissension among team members that had developed as a result of various personality conflicts. Within a week, I succeeded in getting team members to communicate their concerns and resolve their differences. This achievement immediately improved the staff's ability to unify and work as a cohesive team toward the common goal of providing exemplary patient care.

While this is but one of the accomplishments highlighted on my enclosed résumé, I believe it speaks to my effectiveness in a leadership role. My staff would describe me as compassionate and good-natured, but they are also quick to acknowledge my abilities in assessing a situation for what it is and implementing swift measures to resolve the issue. I am confident that I can lead your NICU team to similar success.

I will be in Seacouver on a house-hunting expedition next week and will give you a call on Wednesday to schedule an interview. I look forward to hearing more about your plans for the unit!

Sincerely,

Frank Thompson

Gladys Gavlak
4761 Havern Rd., Monroe, Michigan 48161 ■ (734) 555-9421

March 12, 1998

Search Committee Chair
St. Anne High School
100 W. Main Street
Monroe, MI 48162

This letter is a great example of articulating what benefits Gladys can provide to the employer. She is addressing the needs of the employer, not just highlighting her skills.

Dear Search Committee:

I am pleased to submit the enclosed résumé in consideration for the position of Principal of St. Anne High School. My résumé briefly outlines over 25 years of experience in the educational field (primarily in Catholic education), and 15 years in administration.

As you may know, I have a strong record of commitment to this school. I graduated from St. Anne Academy, and later served as an English Teacher there. Last year, I returned to St. Anne as its Assistant Principal with a renewed sense of enthusiasm, commitment, and purpose.

My goals and vision for St. Anne are:
1. To continue St. Anne's strong tradition of excellence.
2. To nurture and develop Christian values as an integral part of Catholic education.
3. To instruct the whole student – including the student's intellectual, physical, social, moral, and spiritual life.
4. To make further progress toward the target goals for Writing Across the Curriculum, Oral Communication, and Relevancy in Education.
5. To continue to play a key role in the Capital Campaign and the Development Program.

I believe that some of the strengths I can bring to this position are:
- Strong leadership skills, with the ability to provide unity and direction in implementing goals.
- A visible, approachable presence; good rapport with teachers, students, and parents.
- Excellent communication, organization, facilitation, and coordination skills.

I would appreciate the opportunity to meet and share with you on a personal level my commitment to fostering the growth of St. Anne High School and its students. I look forward to hearing from you soon.

Sincerely,

Gladys Gavlak

Enclosure

Beauregard (Bud) Brown

321 East Maine Avenue   (207) 555-2222   Down Home, ME 04000

September 10, 1998

> *This letter, though a little long, is light and in-formal enough to remain interesting. Good personal examples to support the "people person" claim.*

Mr. John Smyth
ABC Communications
987 South Street
Anytown, ME 04001

Dear Mr. Smyth:

Please accept this letter in application for a position as **Public Liaison** with your organization.

I am a "people person." Since my early retirement from our local telephone company last winter, I have had my fill of retirement living, and miss my daily "fix" with the public. Please accept this letter as both a resume and a testimony to my eagerness to assist you in Customer Relations.

For 26 years, I was gainfully employed by Down Home Telecommunications, and have serviced the public in all areas of my work. As an installer and repairman, I have successfully:

- Utilized exceptional interpersonal skills with customers and co-workers, providing service to a diverse range of customers, including large corporate accounts, chief executive officers, small businesses, prisons, the retarded and individuals from all socioeconomic levels. One of my proudest moments was my receipt of a letter of commendation from the Chief Executive Officer of DHT for **outstanding customer service**, prompted by praise from an exceptionally satisfied customer.
- Engaged in both highly technical and complex mechanical work, including conversions from manual wiring to computerized services and maintenance/repair of gasoline engines. My abilities include excellent troubleshooting, problem-solving and analytical skills. My skills rest, in part, on my proven ability to be highly observant, attentive to detail, extremely disciplined and self-reliant.

At DHT, when there was a "problem customer," I was always the technician called to the scene. One co-worker told me, "Bud, you could get along with Attila the Hun!" I have always enjoyed assisting others, whether in technical problem-solving, dealing with paperwork, or teaching co-workers the most efficient way to accomplish a task.

This summer I helped out a friend, serving as General Manager of his small manufacturing firm. In this position, I supervised a dozen workers, scheduled labor and production times, handled all shipping/receiving and cooperated with six vendors to maintain a smooth workflow. Production increased from less than 100,000 parts per week to an average of over 122,000/week in less than two months.

I offer you a unique combination of strong interpersonal, communication, technical and mechanical skills which will help you measurably in your public relations efforts. Could we meet to discuss the ways in which I might enhance your customer satisfaction levels? I eagerly await a call from you to schedule a time for us to speak.

Thank you for your time and consideration of my qualifications.

Sincerely,

Bud Brown

Mark Dalglish
931 South Mission Road, Suite B, Fallbrook, California 92028   310 555-1212

January 7, 1998

Short and easy to read. Concise highlight of qualifications.

Mr. Carl Erznoznik
BCD Corporation
123 Some Street
Fallbrook, California 92028

Dear Mr. Erznoznik:

Please accept this letter and accompanying résumé as evidence of my interest in applying for a Receptionist's position with your company.

My enclosed résumé clearly shows I have qualifying skills and abilities compatible with positions such as this. Briefly, they are:

- more than three years hands-on experience dealing with the public in reception and customer service positions,

- an innate ability to successfully coordinate multiple tasks simultaneously, and

- a sincere desire to contribute to the continued growth and success of your company.

After you have the opportunity to review my résumé I would like to meet with you to discuss how effectively I can contribute. I will call in a few days to arrange such a meeting. Should you have any questions before scheduling an appointment I may be reached through the number listed above.

Thank you very much for taking the time to review my résumé and for your kind consideration. I look forward to speaking with you in the near future.

Sincerely,

Mark Dalglish

Enclosure

Mark Staples

22 Arleen Lane
Centereach, NY 11720
phone / fax 516-555-5555
mstaples@mindspring.com

January 14, 1999

Mr. Tom O'Callaghan
Director of Human Resources
The Gap Regional Office
Crocker Square
2600 North Military Trail, Suite 248
Boca Raton, FL 33431

> *Good use of opening with common acquaintance. Credible, detailed examples of qualifications in the retail field.*

Dear Mr. O'Callaghan:

Your Port Jefferson store manager, Lauren Mitchell, was my colleague at Macy's Northeast a few years ago. Linda knows that I possess the ability to creatively react to today's rapidly changing retail climate while retaining a realistic focus on the bottom line. She suggested that I contact you, as you are advertising for a corporate merchandise manager.

My twelve-year retail career includes experience with Macy's and The Limited, where I was responsible for buying and merchandising functions for ready-to-wear departments and stores, with responsibility for up to $100 million in annual sales. This experience has proven invaluable in today's downsized retail industry where solid management skills in multiple functions have become essential to maximizing productivity and increasing corporate profits.

The following accomplishments are representative of the abilities I can bring to The Gap:

- Achievement of optimal 9X inventory turnover and 11% net profit by effective sales analysis, strategic cost reduction, and tight payroll management.

- Merchandising management for a $100 million, 40-store, ready-to-wear division and a $50 million, specialty chain store division.

- Building of rewarding working relationships with superiors and subordinates by employment of exceptional work ethic, integrity and dedication. My staff works hard because they know I do!

- Retention of solid senior management, retail, and vendor associations that create profitable opportunities.

As an industry veteran, I have long respected The Gap for its fashion leadership, value orientation, and visual presentation standards. I'd like to bring my expertise and my commitment to excellence to The Gap and I look forward to meeting with you to discuss the ways in which I can contribute to the continuing success of your dynamic management team.

Sincerely,

Mark Staples

Enclosure: Resume in traditional and computer scannable versions

— Award-Winning Top Producer —

"...developed a clientele...unparalleled in the Dallas market."
"...Consistently among the top producers, often leading a field of 18 professionals in both written and delivered sales volume."
"...Held in high regard, both personally and professionally, among her peers."
"...A great asset to any sales or service organization."
—D. Byron Buchanan, Sales Manager
Wickes Furniture

Number of pages including this page: 2

Home: 972.555.5549 Work: 817.555.5799 Fax: 972.555.5945

Sanda S. Spitzer

TO: **Mr. Trea Bowman, Corporate Sales Manager**

DATE: **September 19, 1998**

Sales is very productivity oriented, and this letter capitalizes on her sales accomplishments.

Dear Mr. Bowman:

Is this the kind of performer you're looking for in a sales associate?

- Top producer and award winner - Wickes Furniture - 4 years
- Ranked among top producers in company - Becks Furniture - 4 years
- Company top sales performer - J. Sloan Furniture - 2 years

I love selling. You will read in my resume I have a unique career path, as a successful realtor, Co-owner/Sales Support Manager of a heavy equipment auction company and Co-owner/Operations Manager of a profitable cattle and horse ranch. Each has brought its own rewards, but I've found my happiest niche in furniture sales.

Customers enter a fine furniture showroom because they *want* to. They are making some wonderful changes in their lives and I enjoy being a part of it. My ability to determine exactly what the customer wants produces dramatic increases in sales volume for my showroom and my company. I produce sustainable gains in overall revenue by providing the highest quality customer service through dedicated follow-up and ongoing support. My customers come back.

I never lose sight of the fact that my customers are in my showroom to express their own personality and good taste—through my expertise. Recently I assisted a customer with an extensive home redecorating project—it developed into one of my largest sales to date. I spent several exciting hours with my customer going over details of color, pattern, texture and wood. She thanked me when she left for showing her so many lovely pieces. *My customer had been sightless for over 20 years.* That day was one of the most rewarding days of my career.

You will note from my resume my last position was with Beck's Furniture in northern California. I recently "came home" to Dallas to be closer to family and friends. With great respect for your reputation in the industry, I would like to apply my strengths and talent to your goals and would welcome a personal interview to discuss how I can assist you.

Thank you for your time and consideration of the enclosed materials.

Sincerely,

Sanda Spitzer

Resume Following

> *Simple letter outlining accomplishments and goals.*

94 Meadowlark Lane
Minneapolis, Minnesota 55555

(507) 555-5555

June 11, 1998

J. L. Smith
Director of Human Resources
Pulleyn Corporation
28 S. State Street
Rochester, Minnesota 55904

Position of Interest — Tax Preparer or Accountant

Dear Mr. Smith:

For the past nine years I have worked for Big Name Tax Company, and from 1990 to present have overseen fourteen to nineteen tax offices throughout the state. My accomplishments and areas of expertise are outlined on the enclosed resume.

I am exploring opportunities not only in the tax field, but also in other management areas such as general accounting, financial services, human resources, and recruiting of accounting or management personnel. My contributions to the field have been significant, as is evidenced by my focus on bottom line figures and profitability. Outstanding skills in customer and client services, as well as employee motivation and training, have resulted in measurable successes in account retention and expansion, expense reduction and high revenue generation.

Other assets and strengths include sound decision-making, integrity, zest for challenge, and excellent presentation skills. My ability to oversee multiple branches and franchises with ease attests to my overall managerial and organizational style, as well as my emphasis on employee responsibility and empowerment. Obviously, teamwork has been an important component in my vision for success.

I would welcome the opportunity to join a top flight executive team concerned with productivity, quality customer service and managed growth patterns. You will find my salary requirements to be in line with my experience and level of responsibility. I will be contacting your office to set up an appointment to review my past performance and successes in greater detail. I look forward to our conversation.

Sincerely,

Lars Blanning

DONALD A. FISCHER   2213 Oak Drive • Paris, Texas 75473 • (903) 555-2272

FAX

Page 1 of 2

TO: Jacob D. Brown
           President
           Lamar County Board of Education
           (903) 555-2163

Here is a good example of a faxed letter to accompany a faxed resume.

Date: June 13, 1998

Re: Teaching Opportunities — Paris Elementary School

Receiving a bachelor's degree in elementary education last month from Southern Methodist University signaled the achievement of personal and professional goals. Graduating in the top two percent of the class is more cause for celebration.

During the student teaching portion of my degree program, I was able to introduce a variety of teaching methods that included experimental games and cooperative learning activities. These encouraged a free exchange of ideas among students, and produced measurable improvements in classroom participation and knowledge retention.

As a Paris native, I attended your city's schools, and know first-hand the high quality of education they provide. To become a part of this system would be an exciting way to begin a teaching career.

For expediency in considering me for the fall term, I am submitting qualifications by facsimile. However, an original will be sent by mail.

Thank you for your time and interest. I look forward to hearing from you soon.

DAF:

7

Targeted Cover Letters Directed to Executive Recruiters and Employment Agencies

Often in our career design campaign we want to make use of employment professionals including executive recruiters (headhunters) and employment agencies. Once you have determined that a company may be able to assist you and you have identified a person within the organization who can help you, prepare a strong letter and include your resume.

Use the same methodology as in Chapter 6, for targeting a letter to a specific company. You need to complete the same skills assessment as in Chapter 6, and then target your letter toward meeting the needs of the recruiter and ultimately the client.

Executive recruiters and employment agencies are paid by the companies they represent, not by the job candidate. Your job will be to indicate in your letter and resume that you have the key skills and abilities to meet the needs of the client companies. In other words, you want to communicate your value to the agency, hoping that this value matches the skills and qualifications demanded by the recruiter's clients.

Here are 25 tips for working with recruiters.

25 TIPS FOR WORKING WITH EXECUTIVE RECRUITERS

1. Find a comprehensive listing of executive recruiters, those in your geographic region and those national firms that specialize in your industry. The best source of this information is *The Guide to Executive Recruiters* by Michael Betrus (McGraw-Hill).

2. Retained search firms are paid in advance or on an ongoing basis for a search, usually for higher level positions or unique, hard-to-fill positions. Retained searches are conducted for positions such as a pulp and paper expert for Scott Paper or a senior level corporate officer.

3. Contingency firms are paid when the client company hires the candidate. Typical contingency searches are for positions such as sales representative or business manager.

4. Recruiters are paid by the client company, not by you. Don't misinterpret their motivation or loyalty.

5. Executive search firms never charge prospective candidates.

6. Prior to speaking to a recruiter, have a description of your background well thought out and rehearsed.

7. Make sure your background description addresses your education, number of years of experience in your industry, your primary professional discipline, and several key accomplishments.

8. When a recruiter asks you what you want to do, do not appear indecisive or say anything like, "I don't really know."

9. Contact every recruiter in your preferred geographic region, whether they specialize in your industry or discipline or not. They will know what is going on in your region.

10. Contact every recruiter in the country that specializes in your specific industry or discipline. If your area of expertise is finance, accounting, or sales, you may limit it to your region of the country first.

11. Get recruiters to like you. If they like you, they will help you. Also, in order to stay in contact with recruiters who currently have nothing that suits you, try to call with information or leads for *them* as a result of your own research. You'll be giving them something and they'll be more apt to take your calls and help you network.

12. If a recruiter cannot help you immediately, probe further for a networking contact. This is an extremely valuable approach to use with executive recruiters.

13. Have a good resume prepared to send to recruiters. Unless you have a specific reason not to, always send them a resume and cover letter rather than a broadcast letter. They're going to need it anyway, so don't slow down the process.

14. Extend recruiters the same respect you would a hiring manager with whom you are interviewing.

15. If you're targeting a large company that only works with recruiters, find out the name of the recruiting firm from the company. In many cases they will refer you.

16. Do not feel hesitant to ask recruiters for advice. This is their business and they deal with employment searches every day. If you develop a good rapport, invite them to lunch—your treat.

17. You are more attractive employed than unemployed because you appear to be a lower risk. However, in today's business climate recruiters under-

stand that many good people are looking for work. A strong reference from your previous employer will help.

18. Many recruiters have a tougher time finding qualified candidates than finding job orders from companies. Use this to your advantage and try to present yourself as someone of value to the recruiter.

19. Call a recruiter first as opposed to sending an unsolicited letter. This way you can use the letter to reflect a prior phone conversation. Though it builds more work for them, recruiters we interviewed said it is to the candidates' advantage to call first.

20. Try to bring other business or company information to the recruiter. That will help your relationship.

21. Keep in mind that when negotiating your salary through a recruiter, she or he's playing both sides to come to terms. It's usually an easier process on a personal level to negotiate through a recruiter because of the buffer. Just don't forget that the recruiter is trying to get you hired, not necessarily get you the highest salary.

22. Though there are many large national firms, don't overlook smaller recruitment operations. A small firm may be dedicated to one client company that could be your next home.

23. Contact every recruiter described as a generalist. A generalist will take on a variety of searches, one of which may fit your background.

24. Don't be shy about asking recruiters what you should expect while working with them. If they're a quality firm, they'll be happy to walk you through the process.

25. Stay away from any recruiting firm that tries to prevent you from contacting other search firms. No legitimate recruiter will try to work with you on an exclusive basis.

BETH PASTERZ

7980 North Illinois Avenue, Apt. 3B, Raleigh, North Carolina 27606, (919) 555-1212

August 18, 1998

Simple, straightforward letter to recruiter. Unsolicited letters to recruiters should not be long and need to be straight to the point.

Kyle Darden
Senior Recruiting Specialist
The Darden Firm
Post Office Box 5015
Durham, NC 28758

Dear Mr. Darden:

I am writing to express an interest in the Administrative Assistant position for which you are currently recruiting.

As you will note from my enclosed résumé, I have a diverse background supporting business and medical professionals in a variety of settings, including 10 years in the fast-paced, energetic corporate environment at WDW Productions. My secretarial expertise is well documented by my Certified Professional Secretary (CPS) rating, a credential which I enthusiastically maintain through continuous education and training.

Adept at handling difficult situations, I fully understand the need to maintain confidentiality on sensitive issues and communicate with tact and diplomacy. Widely recognized for my competencies in many of the leading business software applications, I am equally at ease working with Word and WordPerfect as well as Excel and Lotus. My most recent typing speed was clocked at 95 wpm with an 85% accuracy rate. I also speed write and take shorthand, which is somewhat of an anomaly in today's highly technical workplace!

In summary, I bring a sense of commitment, dedication, and professionalism to every aspect of my work, and I am confident that my expertise would greatly benefit your organization.

If you believe that my qualifications warrant an interview, you can reach me at (919) 555-1212.

Sincerely,

Beth Pasterz

Tina Fisher

Box 55 Bayside Lane
Aquebogue, NY 11931
(516) 555-5555

January 14, 1999

Ms. Jeanne Richards
Vice President
Tempo Services
1400 Old Country Road
Westbury, NY 11590

> *Letter opens with position sought. Good explanation of skills, critical for this type of position.*

Dear Ms. Richards:

As a skilled secretary and administrative assistant, I have demonstrated expertise in efficient executive and office assistance directly related to over twenty years of experience with CitiBank. I have built a career specializing in dedicated support of my bosses' daily activities and long-term goals. I would like to do the same for your clients.

Comprehensive skills and an ability to work within many different levels of the corporate structure are exceptionally valuable when working with today's "lean and mean" staffing levels. Efficiency, initiative, flexibility, and a quick learning curve—these are the qualities of an administrative assistant who can step into a short-term or long-term position and make an immediate contribution.

As a seasoned professional, I offer proven expertise in aggressive scheduling, business communications, confidential document administration, and time-sensitive assignments. I understand the complexities, subtleties, and procedures necessary to manage an executive's schedule, or the daily operation of an office. I pride myself on my ability to work hard to ensure that my assignments will progress with optimum productivity and minimal confusion.

Maintaining a totally current technological expertise is my passion. I have received extensive training in most office software (including Microsoft Office and WordPerfect), can quickly learn almost anything on a computer, and have developed a talent for repairing equipment before a service call is made. Of course, I am a proficient user of copy machines, fax machines, printers, and electronic mail.

Ms. Richards, I am sure that there are many candidates who can *meet* your requirements. If offered the opportunity to become a member of the Tempo team, I will *exceed* your expectations. I know I can be an asset, making immediate contributions to your client companies. My schedule is flexible, and I am available for daily short-term or long-term positions. I will call you next week, so that we may discuss assignment possibilities.

Sincerely,

Tina Fisher

Enclosure: Resume in traditional and computer scannable versions.

Kirby Hughes

1477 SW 40th Court, Coral Springs, Florida (954) 555-6583

September 12, 1998

> *This broadcast letter allows Kirby to better articulate his experience and career goals.*

Ms. Lori Harding
Robert Half International, Inc.
1450 E. Las Olas
Fort Lauderdale, FL 33444

Dear Ms. Harding:

If you are in search of a senior-level engineering manager for one of your executive searches, you may want to give serious consideration to my background.

Highlights of my experience are:

- M.S. Mechanical Engineering, University of Florida
  B.S. Electrical Engineering, Georgia Tech

- 16 years Engineering and Management experience with:

  - Pratt & Whitney; V.P. Engineering (aircraft division), 4 years
  - IBM; Director of Project Engineering (software interface), 7 years
  - Boeing Corporation; Project Engineer, 5 years

In my current capacity as Vice President for Pratt & Whitney I manage an engineering group of 450 responsible for aircraft motor design in three facilities in the country. This includes engineering design through to process design of manufacturing.

I have established a strong reputation for the quality and quantity of capital project work completed in my department. I have a solid reputation as a demanding and fair leader. The work performed under my direction has come in at or below budget, and we always meet project deadlines.

I have chosen to leave Pratt for personal reasons; they are unaware of my decision. My current compensation is about $130,000. Should you be interested, please contact me at home at (954) 555-6583.

Sincerely,

Kirby Hughes

Phil Ehart

1978 Mariabronn • Lawrence, Kansas 12345
(810) 555-1112 (voice) • (810) 555-1113 (fax) • pehart@kansas.com

> *This broadcast letter format allows the candidate to articulate relevant accomplishments in his discipline.*

August 8, 1998

Don Kirshner, Senior Recruiter
Kirshner & Associates
12 Masque Court
Icarus, Kansas 12345

Dear Mr. Kirshner:

With your expertise in executive placement, you might know of manufacturing companies looking for an experienced and accomplished General Manager, President/Vice President, or Director of Operations. If so, please review my résumé and consider introducing my credentials to them.

When I started as the GM for Norman Products, Inc. seven years ago, I inherited the leadership of a recently purchased food processing plant operating at a $3 million loss with low production rates (63% of budgeted capacity), unscheduled downtime problems (20%), untrained staff, poor safety practices, high turnover (200%), and lack of cooperation between departments. I made the decision to retrain and empower our staff while building accountability, short- and long-term goals, and continuous improvements into the system. Within three years we accomplished quite a bit:

- Doubled production output, reaching 110% of budgeted capacity while capturing 83% of the raw material available via strategic pricing and contract negotiations.
- Increased ROA to 11% as profits approached $24 million.
- Decreased material disposition time from 3.3 weeks to 24 hours.
- Reduced unit production costs (from $.64/lb. to $.33/lb.), unit raw material handling costs (from $.40/cwt to $.14/cwt), and unscheduled downtime (from 20% to 2% range).

These results are verifiable and have set the stage for unprecedented growth expected in the next fiscal year. Please do not hesitate to call if I can provide any additional information that will help you present my qualifications to one of your clients. I have traveled extensively throughout my career and would gladly entertain a challenging position that required either domestic or international relocation.

Thank you for your assistance and reply. I look forward to hearing from you.

Sincerely,

Phil Ehart
enc.

MARY BETH ROSE

9834 Panama Canal Blvd.
Los Angeles, CA 90012
(310) 555-8748

August 6, 1998

Mr. Thomas Chrisp
Senior Partner
Chrisp & Associates
3545 East 45th Street, Suite 201
New York, NY 10118

Very professional letter. Focus is more on skills than accomplishments.

Dear Mr. Chrisp:

In order to compete in today's marketplace an organization must be able to effectively recruit, develop and retain top-performing management, supervisory and line personnel. As a Senior Human Resources Executive for several corporations, I have supported long-term growth, expansion, and diversification based on proven success in:

- Leading innovative recruitment campaigns to identify well-qualified candidates from senior managers to technical staff, often within highly-competitive markets nationwide.
- Reengineering the systems and methodologies to streamline hiring practices, accelerate placement, reduce cost per hire and enhance employee retention.
- Facilitating the successful integration of personnel from autonomous business units, creating a cohesive operating environment despite conflicting management styles and organizational structures.
- Developing customized leadership, executive development and other training programs to capitalize on personnel strengths and maximize human resource utilization.
- Providing decisive leadership to drive organizational change, process reengineering and productivity improvement.

The scope of my experience spans the entire HR function from recruitment, staffing, benefits, HRIS, employee relations, training and development, succession planning, and performance/productivity improvement. Most significant are my efforts in partnering HR with operations, stressing to management the critical impact of its employees upon long-term corporate performance. In turn, I have positioned myself as a key advisor and advocate to top management, translating their objectives into actionable performance plans.

Now, I am confidentially exploring new challenges with an organization in need of decisive recruitment, training and employee development leadership. If you are working with a client company seeking a candidate with my qualifications, I would welcome a personal interview. My goal is to relocate back to the Mid-Atlantic Region and my recent base compensation has averaged $80,000. Thank you for your time and consideration.

Sincerely,

Mary Rose

MANUEL VANCERRO
Wosque de Capuliners 5326, Wosque de las Lomas
147730, Mexico City, D.F.
Tel: 555-555-555-5555 · Fax: 555-555-555-5555
Email: xxxxxxxxx@telmex.net.mx

> *Simple and easy to read—good for recruiter. Quickly conveys interest in multi-national business.*

Ms. Janice Lamonte
CR Association
2567 Maple Avenue
Dallas, Texas 00000
U.S.A.

Dear Ms. Lamonte:

My resume was sent to you within the past 14 days, as I wish to contribute to the success of a US company with business dealings in Latin America.

As an experienced and successful international management/marketing executive, my record includes significant contributions to my employers, including developing profitable new/start-up businesses, directing multi-faceted projects, leading sales/marketing efforts, and successfully launching new products to achieve corporate objectives.

My background includes:

- **Bicultural/bilingual in English and Spanish**
- **Proficiency in multi-cultural business environments and cross-cultural communications**
- **Achieving sales and revenue growth of 25% and 30% respectively for worldwide tourism organization (annual industry revenue of US $5.6 billion)**
- **Winning US $40 million in new contracts for multi-national corporate clients in US and Latin America within 20 months**
- **Building 3 companies from start-up to combined US $11.5 million in annual sales with an average 35% gross profit**

I am again renewing my interest in continuing my career with your assistance, and am enclosing my resume for your review. I look forward to conversing with you, either by email or telephone.

Very truly yours,

MANUEL VANCERRO

Enclosure

SYLVESTER HUNT, P.E.
931 South Mission Road, Suite B, Fallbrook, California 92028 714 555-1884

Accomplishments bulleted directly relate to candidate's discipline. Notice how Sylvester requested confidentiality.

January 7, 1998

Mr. Michael Goga
Goga, Joseph, Schuster and Smith
123 Some Street
Fallbrook, California 92028

Dear Mr. Goga:

After considerable success in my current position, I find myself without an interesting challenge on the horizon. Do you have a client who may be interested in my services?

My enclosed résumé clearly indicates I have a verifiable record of success in increasingly responsible project management assignments. My most recent accomplishments are:

- negotiating a $39.7 million multi-agency funding agreement facilitating completion of 16 miles of Interstate 12 through northern New Mexico

- developing and administering a $28 million Water Bond Certificate of Participation for construction of master planned water facilities in Boxeo County, and

- orchestrating and implementing a seven-year intergovernmental cooperation program designed to provide recycling services throughout the county.

After you have the opportunity to review my résumé I would like to speak with you; I will call in a few days. Should you have any questions before I call, or if you know of a company seeking someone like me, you may reach me through the number listed above.

Please keep my inquiry confidential as I do not want to alarm the rest of the company just by considering alternatives. And, please do not forward my materials to any employer without first discussing the particular opportunity with me.

Thank you very much for taking the time to review my résumé and for your consideration. I look forward to our conversation.

Sincerely,

Sylvester Hunt

Christopher Gladden
846 Blue Ridge Circle, Miami, FL 33335 (305) 555-7893

> *Excellent broadcast letter that positions candidate in a position of professional strength. Accomplishments are very bottom-line oriented.*

June 3, 1996

Mr. John Loureiro
TTS Personnel
420 Lexington Avenue
New York, NY 10170

Dear Mr. Loureiro:

Several of my associates in the communications industry here in South Florida have mentioned you as someone experienced with similar firms in the New York area. We should talk soon.

My experience with sales and distribution of wireless communications products in this market is certainly one of success:

- After I became Regional Sales Manager for Pactel in 1988, we improved our sales by 55% in one year. The sales staff was demoralized, and we improved their training and replaced other staff members. Our market share is up to 22% in just three years.

- We created a selling program locally that resulted in an 18% higher closing rate, and that program was taken on the road to train all other Pactel sales reps.

Unfortunately, all this hard work has caused the company to be acquired. The new brass have indicated a desire to sell off the division I manage. This is a great opportunity for me to return to New York. I will call you next week to discuss possible opportunities in the "Big Apple."

Sincerely,

Christopher Gladden

Hester R. Swann

> Highlights of accomplishments are qualitative, leaving quantitative ones to the resume enclosed. Letter will be easy for recruiter to understand profile of Hester.

8950 Miami Trail
Cincinnati, Ohio 45242
(513) 555-3456
e-mail hrswann@aol.com

August 10, 1998

Jack L. Huntington
Principal
Executive Recruiter Group
8585 New York Street
Stamford, CT 06523

Dear Mr. Huntington:

If one of your clients is in search of a *top performing* sales management professional with a history of leading sales teams to the best records in their history, then we should discuss your client's challenges and what I have to offer.

My accomplishments include:

- A 15-year track record of consistently successful sales and sales leadership — always outperforming sales goals.
- Proven ability to deliver predictable and consistent sales results — steady revenue streams — through outstanding contributions from all members of the sales team.
- Leadership of product development and product launch — contributing a sales and marketing perspective to corporate planning.

In short, I am a leader both by example and through effective management of individuals and teams. I have contributed significantly to sales and profitability for companies in the medical products, pharmaceutical, and retail industries. Personally committed to continued growth and excellence, I have the drive, energy, vision, leadership and implementation skills to make a positive difference to any sales organization.

Are my record and qualifications of interest? Greater detail is supplied in the enclosed resume, and I would be glad to elaborate on any of this information. The enclosed salary history may also be helpful in evaluating my candidacy.

Let's talk soon. I am confident that your clients will be interested in my track record and ability to help them achieve important business goals.

Sincerely,

Hester R. Swann

enclosures

BETTY CHANDLIER
151 W. Passaic Street · Rochelle Park, New Jersey 07662
(201) 555-5555 · Email: bchand@xxxxx.net

Ms. Ellen Derych
Derych & Associates
10 Linda Court · Suite #6
New York, New York 00000

Dear Ms. Derych:

What a pleasant experience it was to discuss your client's opening with you! I appreciate the candid approach that prevailed during our discussion and feel you gave me a comprehensive understanding of the District Sales Manager position. I can see in it an opportunity to apply the sales/staff building techniques I have acquired over the years with Fabrinni, LTD.

You certainly made clear the objectives and responsibilities expected from Gem Corp., involving a rapid and significant increase in volume, addressing client service needs and training/motivating sales staff - all with a cost-conscious approach. I have given considerable thought to the problems and challenges you described and am confident that I can produce the results they expect. My interpersonal skills, leadership abilities and sales/marketing experience will prove advantageous in this respect.

Additionally, please mention to them my store management experience both at Joyce Leslie and Lerner's, which totals over 7 years. At this level, I interacted directly with customers and was accountable for my own sales objectives as well as overall store operations. My ability to train sales associates is approached with a "train by example" technique and it is through my own experience that I am able to develop staff to peak levels.

As you can see, I feel well qualified for the position with Gem Corp., as I am convinced it is just the kind of challenging opportunity I have been seeking. Thank you again for your interest, professionalism, cordiality....and for pointing out all my skills!

Very truly yours,

BETTY CHANDLIER

8

Cover Letters Responding to Classified Advertisements

Fewer than 5 percent of all jobs are ever posted in the classified advertisement section of local, regional, national, and trade publications. Do continually refer to and study the classified advertisements, but don't depend on them or spend more than 5 percent of your time and resources on them. Study each ad and try to identify the specific criteria the employer is seeking in the successful job candidate. Then, in a strong, compelling letter, sell the employer on the fact that you have the skills, experience, and education to warrant an interview and eventual hire.

It is more difficult to answer a blind advertisement because you may not know much about the company or the position. In that case, still try to draw parallels between your skill set and the likely needs of the hiring company.

D ORIS N ELLIS

P.O. Box 895 • Murfreesboro, TN 37133 • (615) 555-3273 tbcprw@AOL.com

August 10, 1998

> *Comprehensive letter reviewing candidate's career aspirations and past experience. Bulleted list in middle focuses on what she can do for the company, not what she is looking for.*

Director of Information Systems
ABC Corporation
P.O. Box 000
Ogden, UT 00000

Dear sir or madam:

Having achieved my goals in my career of public accounting and financial services, I am interested in expanding my professional horizons by seeking new challenges in the direction of applications development and software design. In interest of an opportunity with your organization, I am enclosing my résumé for your consideration.

As you can see, my career in business, finance, and public accounting is extensive. I have enjoyed a reputation as one of the top financial analysts in the country and have been senior executive of an extensive financial services conglomerate. For the past few years, I have had the opportunity to apply my knowledge of these fields in a more technical direction by designing software applications to solve specific needs for clients such as RBC International, Arthur Andersen, and Embassy Corporation. I have a talent and interest in solutions design and business analysis backed by a wealth of practical experience and knowledge of public accounting, business operations, and financial issues. This knowledge has allowed me special insight into developing software that is efficient, cost-effective, and more than satisfactory to the client's needs.

As a team member of your organization, I can provide:

- **Effective applications solutions for financial and business operations**
- **Analysis, needs determination, and project management**
- **Powerful team leadership**
- **Technical instruction and business support for end-users and clients on business issues and application implementation**

With my experience in applications development, I have the knowledge and talent for providing technical solutions for your company. To strengthen my career path further, I am currently pursuing certification as a Microsoft Solutions Developer and am enjoying excellent progress in my studies. My prior business experience coupled with a high level of technical expertise in development and database management is standing me in good stead in my pursuit of formal education in this area.

My objective is to establish a time when we can meet together to discuss how I can add value to your operation. I realize how busy your schedule must be, so I will take it upon myself to be in contact with your office within the next few days to discuss the possibility of an interview. Thank you for your consideration. I look forward to speaking with you soon.

Sincerely,

Doris Nellis

enclosure

BRENT CALLOWAY

123 Fourth St.
Edwards, WI 12345
Telephone: (908) 555-7890

> *Simple introduction letter in response to an advertisement. Last paragraph does a good job of hitting on the real value of that position, and that the candidate understands real business issues.*

Allow me to introduce myself:

For a high volume business environment, a computer glitch can seem like a crisis of cosmic proportions. Neither management nor staff are inclined to wait patiently for a solution; they want someone who will come in and make the problem disappear. That's what I've been doing for over 16 years.

As indicated on the enclosed résumé, I have a broad base of experience prioritizing, integrating, configuring, installing, and maintaining systems for cost effective operations and goal achievement. I have trained and supported both technical and non-technical staff, served as a troubleshooter for software, hardware, and networks, and developed testing and certification standards for various equipment.

In my most recent position, I re-engineered a system so that all of its capabilities were accessible from any computer throughout a large plant, and I made adjustments to give higher resolutions. The results were a much more effective use of the system and increased efficiency at all levels.

Computers should make work easier, not more complicated, and it is my job to see that they do. If you have an opening for a technical professional with a commitment to making problems disappear, I'd like to explore the possibility of employment with your company. Thank you.

Sincerely,

Brent Calloway

Enclosure

WILMA D. DEVINE

3256 Southwest 7th Court, West Palm Beach, FL 33408 (561) 555-7680

> I am a little pencil in the hand of a writing God who
> is sending a love letter to the world.
> — Mother Teresa

September 24, 1999

Mrs. Harriet Mendleson, Program Director
Hospice of Palm Beach County
5300 East Avenue
West Palm Beach, FL 33412

Introductory quote is unique and a real attention grabber. The middle section comparing the required criteria and her credentials is a very good format for answering advertisements.

Dear Mrs. Mendleson:

It is with great interest that I respond to your advertisement in the <u>Palm Beach Post</u> for Director of Volunteer Services for the Hospice of Palm Beach County. I have enclosed my resume for your review and consideration.

I am a fortunate individual who was able to stay home and raise two wonderful children who are now in college. Over the past 20 years, I was active in community service and was always involved with one cause or another. My resume clearly indicates the extent of my involvement. Your advertisement was very specific in what you were seeking:

Your Criteria for Employment	*My Credentials*
* Ten years experience in volunteer work	* Over 15 years in volunteer work
* Five years personnel training & development experience	* Nine years training & development experience
* Strong networking, interpersonal, and leadership skills	* Solid networking and relationship-building skills
* Fundraising experience	* More than ten years experience in fundraising
* College degree preferred	* B.A. from FAU in Communications

I am very much aware of what the Hospice of Palm Beach County means to this community and the important role you play with life and death issues. I attended your "Lifeline Auction," last year and volunteered to help. I was impressed with the turnout of people and the money you were able to raise.

As you can see, I am an admirer of the late Mother Teresa. She once said that "The biggest disease today is not leprosy or tuberculosis, but rather the feeling of being unwanted." As the Director of Volunteer Services, I would work endlessly with your staff to assure that all who need help get it and never feel unwanted or unloved.

If you believe, as I do, that my qualifications and experience would greatly contribute to your organizational goals and objectives, I would welcome the opportunity of introducing myself and my credentials to you in a personal interview to further evaluate if an employment opportunity might be mutually beneficial. Please expect my telephone call in the coming week to arrange such a meeting or you may call me at anytime at the number noted above.

Sincerely,

Wilma D. Devine

DIANE C. VERRO, LPN
266 Highland Street
Bangor, ME 04523

LPN's
Is Your Job a Prison Sentence?

Try something new! EMSA Correctional Care has positions available in the medical unit at Bangor Correctional Facility.

Successful candidates must have ...
- 2 years LPN experience
- State of Maine licenser
- Valid driver's license
- Excellent professional references

Send resume to:
Human Resources Manager
EMSA Correctional Care
PO Box 23900
Bangor, ME 04517
An equal opportunity employer

September 24, 1999

Dear Human Resources Manager:

My job is not a prison sentence because I feel whenever I am making a difference in the lives of my patients, I am in a satisfying and rewarding environment. However, I would like more challenge and I believe your organization might have the kind of challenge I am seeking.

I have had two employers since I completed my formal education, and they are Maine General Hospital and Bangor Medical Center. In both positions as LPN, I was/am recognized for five major achievements over the past eight years:

1) **A perfect attendance record - no absences in eight years**
2) **Going the extra mile to assist physicians, nurses, patients, and staff to provide quality care**
3) **Strong LPN medical skills - committed to continuous improvement**
4) **A great sense of humor; a team player with an outgoing personality**
5) **In-service and homecare experience**

I would like to meet with you personally to formally introduce myself and my excellent references. I can make myself available anytime it is convenient for you with just minimal notice. I thank you for reviewing my qualifications and hope I can become a contributing member of your professional staff.

Sincerely,

Diane C. Verro, LPN

Shannon Alexander

This is a very high energy letter. Though it borders on being too strong, it is interesting to read and a good example of how to talk to the company in a letter.

Washington Avenue
Peoria, IL 61111
(309) 555-1111

June 12, 1999

Mark Johnson, Sales Manager
Randall Pharmaceuticals
P.O. Box 1234
Peoria, IL 61111

Dear Mr. Johnson:

When I saw your ad I thought, "Hold all the résumés, I'm the Pharmaceutical Sales Representative you're looking for!"

You want someone with sales experience. As a consultant for beauty supply houses I took over a territory with sagging sales and began calling on salons. The competition was fierce, but I kept calling, implementing promotional strategies, and providing first class service. Within just a short while I built a loyal clientele and turned the territory around.

You want someone with a knowledge of pharmaceuticals and the medical industry. In addition to several years experience as a pharmaceutical technician, I have lived in Peoria for 13 years. I know area physicians and the local medical community very well. I even know when there's a new doctor in town!

You want a college degree, I have two: a bachelor's in education and an associate's in pharmacology. You want someone to work part time, and that's exactly what I'm looking for. And, I won't be looking for a position with more hours.

In addition to all of the above, I have a high level of energy and a personal commitment to providing the highest level of service. One supervisor, describing my ability to balance multiple assignments in a fast paced environment, dubbed me the "Energizer Bunny." I don't think I could be more suited to the position you advertised. When may we meet for a personal interview?

Sincerely,

Shannon Alexander

Enclosure

RICHARD A. IRELAND
9615 North Union Boulevard
Colorado Springs, CO 80909
(719) 555-9050

August 3, 1998

> *The reference to the specific advertisement is a good idea. Paragraph three articulates key points that would be covered in the enclosed resume.*

Human Resource Manager
P. O. Box 67123
Denver, CO 80131-6712

Re: Restaurant Manager classified advertisement, Denver Post 8/2/98

Dear Human Resource Manager,

Recently I have been looking for a dynamic and challenging position where I can utilize my expertise in the Restaurant/Bar industry and your advertisement seems to offer such an opportunity.

I have enclosed a copy of my résumé, which outlines my qualifications and credentials for Restaurant Management positions and I appreciate your taking the time to review it.

You will note that I have an extensive background in the restaurant and bar industry and have successfully opened restaurants in Colorado, New Mexico, Arizona and Texas. Opening these facilities required expertise in recruitment, interviewing, training and motivation. I also believe it is important to note that no fewer than 5 employees under my direct supervision and training have been promoted to management positions within my present organization. Lastly, I also maintain excellent relationships with numerous food and beverage distributors here in Colorado and have experience in negotiating vendor prices.

My success in the past has stemmed from my strong commitment and sense of professionalism I maintain high ethical and work standards for myself and have excellent rapport with customers, vendors and employees.

I look forward to receiving a telephone call requesting a personal interview so that we might discuss the strengths I can bring to your company.

Sincerely,

Richard A. Ireland

Enclosure: Résumé

WILLIAM R. COTY
2466 Aikens Park Ave.
Jupiter, FL 33420
(561) 555-8827

SCHOOL BUS DRIVERS
Full & Part Time

If you enjoy working with children, have a good driving record, can pass a physical examination, and are interested in employment during the school year (180 student days), we will train you to operate a school bus.
****
Base pay is $7.75/hr. With incentive bonuses based on attendance, driving, safety record. Must have excellent references, a clean record, and project a neat and professional image.
****
Send resume to: P.B.C. School District, Dept. of Personnel, 3300 Forest Hill Blvd., WPB, FL 33406
An equal opportunity employer

Scanned newspaper advertisement is a good idea. Reference from high profile employer is a good attention grabber as well, and lends credibility to the applicant.

William Coty is one of the most dependable, safety-oriented individuals I have ever employed. His driving record is impeccable and his interpersonal skills are extraordinary.

Carl R. Dennison, G.M. Airborne Express

June 11, 199

Dear Personnel Manager:

In addition to exceeding your requirements for School Bus Driver as advertised in the Palm Beach Post, Sunday, June 9th, I have two children in the Palm Beach School System and know the critical importance of child safety. I am seeking a part-time driving position and have enclosed my resume for your review.

I work full-time as a Driver for Airborne Express - on the second shift (4 PM to Midnight). I can work mornings on a regular basis and fill in as needed in the early afternoon, as well as on weekends if the needs exists. I have also enclosed five letters of reference from former employers/bosses.

In closing, I hope you consider my qualifications as School Bus Driver. I am seeking a long-term relationship and hope you will see the merit in investing in me.

Sincerely,

William R. Coty

Paul Preclighter
931 S. Mission Road, Suite B, Fallbrook, California 92028 ● 555-1212

January 7, 1998

This illustrates a basic letter format responding to a newspaper advertisement.

Mr. Michael Joseph
Littlbey Corporation
123 Slothome Street
Fallbrook, California 92028

Dear Mr. Joseph:

I am writing in response to your recent advertisement soliciting résumés for the Security Director's position. Please accept this letter and accompanying résumé as evidence of my interest in applying for that position with your company.

My enclosed résumé clearly shows I have qualifying skills and abilities compatible with this position. Briefly, they are:

- Considerable industry-related experience augmented by a formal education and refined by specialized training,

- A proven record of success achieved through diligence, hard work, attention to detail, and my belief in a consistent application of the fundamentals, and

- A sincere desire to contribute to the continued growth and success of your company.

After you have the opportunity to review my résumé I would like to meet with you to discuss how effectively I can contribute. Should you have any questions before scheduling an appointment I may be reached through the number listed above.

Thank you very much for taking the time to review my résumé and for your kind consideration. I look forward to speaking with you in the near future.

Sincerely,

Paul Preclighter

Enclosure

SHAWN WILLIAMS

Home: (309) 555-1111 • Business: (309) 555-2222 • Mobile: (309) 555-3333

5698 Northmore Road • Peoria Heights, Illinois 61111

> *Simple introduction letter in response to an advertisement. Last paragraph does a good job of hitting on the real value of that position, and that the candidate understands the real business issues.*

Allow me to introduce myself:

In every position I've held, I have been called upon to resolve customer and personnel problems, implement training programs, penetrate new markets, and generally bring order out of chaos. My title has been Service Manager, Sales Representative, and Inspector, but what I really am is a fire fighter.

As indicated on the enclosed résumé, I have 15 years progressive experience in all aspects of outside sales, sales management, and customer support. In my current job I oversee all sales and service activities for a rapidly growing pest control business, with responsibility for profitability, compliance, the management of several routes, and the training and motivation of a diverse staff. In addition to numerous awards, I have been consistently recognized for my ability to build long-term customer loyalty, and for my skills in managing multiple simultaneous responsibilities.

I have never been a maintainer. I enjoy taking on a challenge, resolving problems, and being a part of the growth of a business. If you are seeking someone with a track record of putting out fires and improving service levels, I'd like to explore the possibility of employment with your company. Thank you.

Sincerely,

Shawn Williams

Enclosure

Andrew Taylor

142 Fifth Avenue ☞ Washington, IL 61111
(309) 555-1111 ☞ Andrew@aol.com

Notice how Andrew writes almost as if he is talking, allowing his personality to show through. This demonstrates a good balance of maintaining professionalism and personality.

To Whom It May Concern:

High school can be a pivotal time – at least that was the case in my life! It was either waste four years or discover that learning can be worthwhile, and even fun. I credit a few good teachers for helping me make the breakthrough.

As a student teacher, and more recently a substitute, I have enjoyed the challenge of making learning an exciting and enjoyable process. This doesn't mean that I create a "carnival" atmosphere, however. For my first day in each class, I begin in a serious manner so that students are on their guard, and I gradually incorporate creative projects. The result has been a positive and open environment without any resulting loss of control.

I have incorporated mock courtrooms, cooperative learning research groups, and skits of historical figures. Students seem to enjoy being in my class, and there is no question I enjoy teaching. As you will see, I have also had additional supervisory and counseling experience at Camp Winnamac for the past two years, which has served to round out my teaching abilities. I am very interested in acquiring a full time teaching position where I will be able to use my education and talents to make a difference in the lives of young people.

May we meet for an interview? I would welcome the opportunity to learn more about your school, and to present my qualifications in person. I guarantee you won't be disappointed!

Thank you for your time and professional courtesy in reviewing the enclosed résumé. I look forward to speaking with you soon.

Sincerely,

Andrew Taylor

Enclosure

9

The Broadcast Cover Letter

The broadcast letter is a hybrid between a resume and a cover letter. It is used when you do not wish to convey your full credentials via a resume right out of the box.

When do you use a broadcast letter? There are many instances when a broadcast letter will be effective in generating initial interest in a candidate. The broadcast letter looks more like a letter than a resume, so the reader may be apt to give it a bit more attention. This is especially true when a screening authority (secretary or administrative assistant) is screening material for her or his boss. They are more apt to pass on a letter to the boss but might more readily redirect a resume to personnel or human resources.

Suppose you are employed but do not want to take any chances that your current employer will find out you are looking for a job. Certainly you will not want to send out a resume that names your current employer. This would be a good time to consider creating a broadcast letter.

The broadcast letter may limit the amount of sizzle compared to your resume, or it may hold more sizzle. The broadcast letter is an exercise in creativity (more so than the resume) and needs to be written very well or the strategy can backfire and become disadvantageous.

The only downside of a broadcast letter is that it may not fit into that recruiter or human resource person's mold of a resume or cover letter. Some recruiters feel it only slows down the process, because they will need to see the resume anyway. Try to direct the broadcast letter to targeted companies rather than to executive recruiters.

MICHELLE-ROSE LEMAY
99 Reddington Street
Swampscott, MA 10970
(781) 555-0192 Home
(781) 555-0193 Fax

September 29, 1999

Mrs. Barbara Davis, Editor
Boston Magazine
81 Boylston Street
Boston, MA 10922

> *Highlights key strengths and employment background.*

Dear Mrs. Davis:

I have a solid record for bringing in advertising dollars to prestigious, up-scale publications from Aspen, Beverly Hills, and Palm Beach, to Newport, RI and San Diego. As a "top producing" sales professional, I am certain I can be a contributing member of your advertising sales team.

Key Strengths

* Presentation and closing skills
* Graphic art and production management
* Customer service & retention management

* Networking; building key alliances
* Concept development
* High ethical/professional standards

Past Employment - 1985 - 1999

Aspen Monthly, Aspen, CO	**Sales Supervisor**
Beverly Hills Illustrated, Beverly Hills, CA	**Sales Associate**
The LaJolla Magazine, San Diego, CA	**Sales Associate**
Palm Beach Illustrated, Palm Beach, FL	**Advertising Sales Associate**
The Newport News, Newport, RI	**Sales Associate**

I would like to stop by and introduce myself and share my portfolio to you. Would next week be convenient? I will contact you this Thursday at 11:00 AM to determine if such arrangements would interest you.

Thank you for your time and consideration.

Sincerely,

Michelle-Rose LeMay

URSULA N. MORRIS
2524 Santa Monica Blvd.
Los Angeles, CA 90021
(222) 555-0996

October 19, 1999

Joel Pels, Program Director
Greater Los Angeles Jewish Community Center
1818 Wilson Road
Los Angeles, CA 90022

Dear Mr. Pels:

Notice the lead with achievements ahead of everything else, followed by education. For this type of employment, that is frequently more important than employment history.

Joanne Green provided me with your name and thought it might be beneficial if we got together and discussed your Cultural Arts programs.

I set up the Cultural Arts program at the JCC in Marblehead, MA and today, 10 years after its inception, the program is considered one of the best in the country. I would like to make your Cultural Arts program the benchmark for all others to emulate. Below are a few career highlights:

Achievements
Leadership role in successful start-up of Marblehead JCC Cultural Arts program
Recipient of Irving Cohen Award for Outstanding Achievement in Program Development
Awarded JCC Program Director of the Year
First full-time Cultural Director for School of the Arts, Salem, MA

Education
Master of Education   Boston University
Bachelor of Arts in Education   Northeastern University
Certificate of Achievement, Jewish Studies   University of Tel Aviv

Past Employment
Program Developer/Director   JCC Marblehead, MA
Director - Cultural Arts   School of the Arts
Fund-raiser / Volunteer Supervisor   American Cancer Institute

If you believe, as I do, that my qualifications and credential merit further review on how I can best serve your community center's cultural needs, I would appreciate the opportunity of meeting with you. Please expect my telephone call in the coming week to arrange such a meeting. Thank you for your consideration.

Sincerely,

Ursula N. Morris

Patrick E. Robertson

300 Pine Wood Way
Greenwich, CT 06830
residence ● 203-555-5555

office ● 212-000-000
residence fax ● 203-000-0000
e-mail ● perwan@aol.com

January 14, 1999

Ms. Robin Siegal
President, Cerion Technologies
1401 Interstate Drive
Champaign, IL 61822-1065

> *Very strong and professional letter. This type of letter allows Patrick to explain and sell his accomplishments, where his resume would be written in a more terse manner.*

Dear Ms. Siegal:

Today's financial leaders will be integral strategists in the profitable growth of complex corporate entities as they move into the Year 2000 marketplace. If you have a need for a visionary senior-level executive with a cross-functional background in general corporate finance, start-ups, joint venture negotiations, and public/private financing, we should talk.

As current Vice President of Finance for a Fortune 500 industrial leader, and former CFO of two mid-sized manufacturers, I have been instrumental in the origination of highly imaginative *and* highly profitable financial management programs achieved through motivational leadership blended with sound financing and creative thinking.

The following accomplishments reflect the absolute value that I can bring to Cerion's current and long-term business ventures:

- The creation of a financial model instrumental in the development of an $85 million, multi-division company from a down-trending $14 million Northeast manufacturing business.

- The negotiation and closing of an exclusive joint-venture agreement and the development of a manufacturing subsidiary, each individually representing $300 million in potential sales.

- The procurement of $10 million in below-prime financing for a 500,000 square foot manufacturing facility.

- The establishment of internal credit corporations that turned a $2 million profit in two years.

If you are looking for a senior manager who will make an immediate and positive impact upon operations, revenue streams, and profit margins, I would like to explore the opportunity. I look forward to speaking with you soon.

Sincerely,

Patrick E Robertson

Enclosure: Resume in traditional and computer scannable versions.

Good opening by mentioning common acquaintance. Overall, this is a very strong letter overviewing his qualifications and potential contributions.

ANTHONY T. ROBERTS
122 Dunn Park Road, #23
Rochelle Park, NJ 07662
(201) 555-KEYS

November 4, 1999

Mr. Robert C. Haynes, Manager
SOS Locksmith
8995 South Main Street
Rochelle Park, NJ 07664

Dear Mr. Haynes:

Glenda Williams, probation officer for Meekham County gave me your name and suggested I call you. I am a highly experienced locksmith, and though I have no formal training, there is very little I don't know about the business. In fact, I am working with Glenda because I became too good at my trade.

Glenda told me that you work with people who have experienced some trouble with the law ONLY if they are committed to total rehabilitation and work hard to get ahead. I have a wife and three children. I made a horrific mistake two years ago and will never do anything to jeopardize my future again.

I offer you the following:

1)   Strong credentials - electric locks and access control to automobile and household locks
2)   Commercial and residential work
3)   Security work - dead bolts, GM Vats System, high security locks and upgrades
4)   Master key systems, keyless locks, and safe/combination experience

License and Certification:

I was told by Glenda that when employed and after 90 days of "above-average" performance, I will be eligible, at the State's Expense, to enroll me in a certification program that will result in State licenser. I am committed to attaining this credential.

Integrity and Customer Service Orientation:

Finally I promise to abide by all your organizational policies and procedures and assure you that I bring integrity to the job and will do whatever it takes to serve the customer.

I will be meeting with Glenda next Monday at 10:00 AM and will plan to call you from her office. If you need any further information about me, Glenda suggested you call her at 555-4672 EXT. 27. I thank you for your time and trust in Glenda and me. I will not let you down!

Sincerely,

Anthony T. Roberts

RICHARD H. VAN BURGUEN
4419 Sylvan Glen , Fairport, New York 14450
(555) 555-5555 · dhvb@eznet.net

Mr. Ralph Dixon, CEO
ABC Company
345 Main Street
New York, New York 10023

> *This letter contains virtually all of the key information a resume contains. Very intensive letter and information-rich.*

Dear Mr. Dixon:

Recognized as a dynamic management executive, I possess a career in successfully building and leading companies to profitability and growth. My expertise includes new business development, strategic sales and marketing campaigns, team leadership and operational management. Thoroughly versed in all aspects of business acceleration and experienced in business turnaround, I am considered a change agent capable of taking a company to sustained growth well into the twentieth century.

For the past three years, I have served as Vice President for Sales and Marketing of Ramco Products, a multi-million dollar packaging and material-handling company, with sales throughout North America and expansion negotiations with Europe and Central America. I was recruited to plan and implement an aggressive sales and marketing plan to establish worldwide sales and capture international sales: under my tenure, revenue has increased by 70% with a 225% growth rate for a plastic packaging product.

Prior, I served as the Vice President, Sales and Marketing for Prevent Care, a multi-million dollar preventive maintenance company servicing U.S. commercial fleets. Accountable for marketing, sales and partnering with key accounts, I led my team in reengineering the company's strategies and we grew revenue more than 200% while fostering alliances with 3 new partners.

I served as the Vice President of Marketing with Sensi-Electronics Corp., (an $800 million electronic loss prevention technology corporation, operating domestically and internationally), where I was accountable for directing the operations of the North America industrial and retail businesses ($550 million). I successfully identified and captured new business through aggressive marketing tactics, including opportunities valued at $2 billion, and generated 15% incremental revenues. We were successful in differentiating the company from the competition by launching a technology protection program incorporating selling integrated systems vs. stand-alone commodity closed-circuit television products.

I launched my career with the worldwide leader in document solutions, Xerox Corp., and earned a series of fast-track promotions during a period of aggressive growth and expansion, and advanced to the position of Manager, Market Strategies. As a member of the company's key task force, I contributed to the strategy accountable for expanding reprographic marketshare from 13% to 26%.

I hold a B.B.A. in Marketing and stay current in today's dynamic business climate through continual training.

Dynamic, results-oriented and highly motivated, I look forward to speaking with you and will contact you in the next 10 days to discuss your needs in greater detail.

Very truly yours,

RICHARD H. VAN BURGUEN

Jennifer A. Larcom

32 Ocean Drive, Avalon, NJ 08005

voice 609.555.5555 ▪ fax 609.000.0000 ▪ JAL001@aol.com

January 14, 1999

Mr. John Kroll
Vice President of Sales
Barr Laboratories
2 Quaker Road
Pomona, NY 10970

> *Notice how Jennifer opens with key sales accomplishments and then moves on to more discipline-related accomplishments.*

Dear Mr. Kroll:

Do you have a need for an experienced medical/pharmaceutical sales specialist with an award-winning track-record in revenue development, relationship management, product launches, and training?

As a medical/pharmaceutical account manager and area trainer, managing a $5.5 million New York metro-region territory, I offer quantifiable expertise directly related to an eighteen-year background with Beecham Laboratories, a Fortune 200 leader in health care solutions.

In recent years, I have produced over $18 million in sales in only 48 months, have attained three Beecham "Quota Buster" awards, and have been appointed to Beecham's prestigious "Presidential Team." Customers appreciate my extensive product knowledge, training abilities, and thorough follow-up. Beecham has recognized my creative marketing, innovative product launches, and comprehensive new-hire mentoring.

Representative accomplishments in specific medical/pharmaceutical areas include:

Anesthesia
Instrumental in converting ten hospitals to Ultane™, a $180/bottle inhalation gas replacing a $20/bottle product. Strategized and implemented creative methods to out-compete big budget companies, create brand awareness, and clearly demonstrate benefits and return-on-investment.

Pharmacy/Nursing
Converted 100% of accounts to Addvantage™, an innovative mixable drug delivery system that replaced a traditional, less effective admixture system. Overcame issue of additional acquisition costs by demonstrating product's savings in labor costs and dramatically reduced medication waste.

Nursing/Surgery
Introduced, educated, and converted 100% of hospital accounts to Beecham's leading-edge PCA (Patient Controlled Analgesic) system. Overcame major resistance in urban area hospitals regarding drug abuse misconceptions, and demonstrated product's many cost savings and patient satisfaction/therapy benefits.

Pharmacy
Launched and sold Beecham's new, generic One Choice Injectables™ to 100% of accounts while competing with multiple companies selling a similar generic line.

Jennifer A. Larcom   page 2

Materials Management/Nursing
Sold Beecham's needleless IV connection/protection systems to all Beecham accounts and three competitive accounts. Packaged concept with training and consultation to improve efficiency and compete against competitor's systems.

Proprietary Co-marketing
Participate in leading-edge co-marketing/sales partnerships with Upjon, Hoechst Marion Roussel, and Purdue Pharma to replace existing medical practices with more effective proprietary antiemetic, oncology, and pain management therapies.

Selling to, and servicing the needs of, urban, suburban, and acute care facilities, I interface with decision-makers from the "basement to the boardroom" — Hospital Administrators, Directors of Pharmacy, Directors of Materials Management, Quality Assurance Professionals, Central Supply Supervisors, Bio-medical Managers, Nursing Supervisors, and specialists of all descriptions.

As is common in the industry, I manage my territory from a non-corporate satellite location, where I must be self-directed and personally accomplish all aspects of sales, sales support, marketing, and in-service/new-hire training. This type of sales requires complete organization, many eighteen-hour days, and total dedication to sales goal achievement and customer care.

Maintaining a totally current expertise is my passion. I regularly update my medical, sales, and computer knowledge through continuous professional development, including 26 Beecham-sponsored certification courses and 21 credits in registered nursing program courses at Brookdale Community College. I hold a Bachelor of Arts and a Paralegal certificate from Monmouth College.

Facing challenging responsibilities with creative dynamism centered on innovation and profit is my fundamental focus. I'd like to meet and discuss the ways in which I can contribute my experience and energy to Barr Laboratories' bottom-line. I will phone next week, and look forward to speaking with you.

Sincerely,

Jennifer A. Larcom

CHRISTOPHER J. HART

123 Dolphin Cove, Orlando, Florida 33980
(407) 555-1212 — CJHart@aol.com

August 18, 1998

Danilo Louega
Director of Human Resources
DSI Corporation
Post Office Box 1818
Orlando, FL 33988

Dear Mr. Louega:

A few months ago, I completed the sale of Thurner Industries, Inc., a company that, in four years of leadership, I successfully turned into a highly profitable and much desired operation. Although I have been offered a similar role for another subsidiary of Thurner Companies, I would like to explore career opportunities building technology-based organizations. In anticipation of opportunities you may have for a Senior Operations or Manufacturing Executive, I enclose my résumé for your consideration. Recent accomplishments include:

- Significant turnaround of Thurner Industries, resulting in a 2300% increase in profitability and successful sale to the industry leader.

- Intense process and quality control re-engineering effort, which led to ISO 9001 certification and a 90% improvement in procedure compliance.

- Launch of a massive facility expansion and operational streamlining initiative, which boosted sales 70%.

As my achievements demonstrate, one of my greatest strengths lies in my ability to take a new or floundering operation and nurture it quickly into profitability. Throughout my career I have successfully applied the principles of growth management, staff development, and business administration to real-life corporate issues. The cornerstones of my management philosophy are excellent communication, team spirit, training, and motivation.

Be advised that my recent compensation has averaged $200,000+, but my requirements are flexible, depending upon location, job responsibilities, and other factors.

As a follow-up to this correspondence, I will call you next week to determine if my qualifications meet your needs at this time. As I have not yet discussed my plans with Thurner, I would appreciate your discretion in this matter.

Sincerely,

Christopher J. Hart

CLIFF W. O'BRIEN

16 North Street, Richmond, VA 26533, (804) 555-7733

> *The focus on the key employers and clients lends infinite credibility to the candidate.*

August 29, 1999

Mr. Holland L. Regal, President
Beltway Technologies, Ltd.
6300 Hunter Way
Waltham, MA 12197

Dear Mr. Regal:

I spearheaded the successful turnaround of three Fortune 100 companies and nine nationally recognized firms since 1981. Though my name is not a household word nor have I been CEO, COO or president of any of the organizations that I have help rehabilitate, I have been the strategic financial tactician behind some of the most successful re-engineering efforts in the past quarter-century in high-tech environments.

Your executive recruiting firm is recognized worldwide as the leader in helping top corporations secure visionary leaders and senior-level executives. Following 17 years of consultative prominence with three of the nations leading consulting firms, I would like now to identify a company that would be interested in my leadership qualities on a long-term basis in a top position as President, CEO, COO, or CFO.

Three employers over the past 17 years

* Arthur Anderson   * Mackenzie & Associates   * Corporate Dynamics International

Twelve notable client companies (accompanied by outstanding references) that I have consulted for:

General Electric	Hewlett Packard	Cisco Systems	Compaq Computer
Intel	Softkey International	GBC	Digital Equipment
Delta Airlines	Lucent Technologies	LaserTools, Inc.	Ford Motor Company

My educational qualifications

MBA Stanford University, 1980
Bachelor of Science: Industrial Engineering / Business Management, Tufts University
Faculty Staff Member: Peter Drucker Worldwide Training and Educational Academy

O'Brien   *Page Two*

Maximizing shareholder earnings / growth management / financial integrity

These are the three critical strengths I bring to the table. I am well-connected with Wall Street and have been personally involved with positioning three companies in the past four years to go public (including drafting a 230-page financial summary and pro forma). Finally, I have spent 60% of my time over the last five years in the international, global arena - helping position companies to maximize foreign market potential.

****

Certainly I do not want to waste precious time for either of us. Should you feel that you might come across a client seeking executive-level leadership that could take advantage of my qualifications and verifiable track record, feel free to contact me and I will forward a detailed, highly confidential resume with supporting documentation. I would be seeking a position with a minimum compensation package of $200,000 and equity stock options based on performance.

Thank you for taking the time to review this letter. I look forward to hearing back from you if you feel an opportunity might exist that would benefit one of your client companies.

Sincerely,

Cliff W. O'Brien

JOHN W. ERICKSON

56 Northhampton Avenue
Woodstock, VT 54333
802.555.2323

April 16, 1999

Ms. Jayne Lourdes
The Dexter Corporation
123 Main Street
Windsor, CT 06095

> *Well written and good examples of accomplishments. Sales accomplishments should always be conveyed in a quantitative manner.*

Dear Ms. Lourdes:

If your staff could benefit through the addition of an eminently qualified senior sales professional, then I suggest it could prove to our mutual benefit to establish a dialogue. While secure in my present post, I am confidentially exploring new opportunities to which I could increase my span of control and have a greater contribution to overall sales results.

As my background reflects, my track record of performance demonstrates consistent advancement in the sales field over the past 14 years within the high-tech and prototype manufacturing environments. In each of my positions, I have eclipsed every previous year's performance by a significant percentage. This has been achieved through opening new markets in competitive arenas, successfully positioning product brands on a worldwide scale, and conducting baseline qualitative/quantitative market research that allows for effective strategic planning and program implementation. This experience should prove highly transferable to your organization. Of specific note may be the following indicators of the sales results I've produced for my employers:

- Implemented strategic selling practices which directly increased previous 2–3% annual growth rate to consistent double-digit percentages *annually* for the past 6 years in highly competitive field.
- Successfully negotiated first-time multi-year contract with major pharmaceutical manufacturer representing 15% in annual revenues to company; secured ranking as #1 sales account executive corporate-wide.
- Effectively turned around annual sales loss of 13% to growth in excess of 35% per year in Pacific Rim markets through innovative product positioning and packaged-solution selling strategies.

I'm confident that these are the types of results I could quickly produce for your company as a senior sales manager. I look forward to the opportunity of discussing your hiring objectives and my qualifications in a personal interview and will contact you to arrange a convenient time. Thank you for your consideration.

Sincerely,

John W. Erickson

Charming opening. In this brief letter, all relevant information is able to be conveyed and articulated relative to her desire to obtain the teaching position.

DANIELLE LAROUCHE

9 Rue de la Chaise
75007, Paris, France
(000) 55-55-55-555
Pariscoach@euronet.net

May 29, 1999

Dr. Arthur G. Cane
University of Massachusetts
1900 College Way
Amhurst, MA 12198

Dear Dr. Cane:

Bon jour, and thank you for taking my call last week. It was a pleasure speaking with you and I am excited about the prospects of joining your teaching staff - to challenge students to learn and appreciate our beautiful language. It would be a highly rewarding experience for us - the students, your department, and me. Below are some of my career highlights and qualifications for your reference.

Education:
The Sorbonne, Paris, France
Baccalaureate Language and History, 1986
Doctorate in Language and History, 1990

Teaching Experience:
Berlitz School of Languages, Paris France, 1988-94
Lead Instructor / Curriculum Development

Paris School for Language Study, Paris, France, 1994 - Present
Vice President / Lead Instructor

Partial Listing of Key Awards and Recognitions:
Figaro Honorarium for Improved Skills in Language Sciences, 1999
Scholastic Advancement Award, Paris Center for Academic Achievement, 1998
LaMonde High Achievement Award, 1995, 1996, 1997
Academic Medal Achievement, Berlitz School of Languages, 1991, 1992, 1993, 1994

I will forward to you my academic credentials and portfolio and was told by the university that they will go out early next week. I will follow up. I will then contact you at the end of the month to arrange next steps. Once again, thank you for considering my candidacy for your Department at U. Mass. I look forward to becoming a member of your fine staff.

Merci and au revoir,

Danielle LaRouche

10
Concept Marketing Letter

The concept marketing letter is a new, exciting, and highly effective type of career design or job search letter that reflects successful strategies and techniques used in direct mail and direct marketing letters. The letters look more like business letters, with headings, quotes, and accentuations to effectively direct the reader to critical information. The main idea of the concept, in addition to its stylish format, is to develop a theme for the letter (teamwork, profit generation, quality control, and so on) and base the entire letter around the theme. If you can identify the key concept (theme) that each prospective employer is looking for and your letter addresses that concept, your resume *and you* will stand out from the sea of other candidates.

DONALD P. LARKIN
18 Forest Lane
Atlanta, GA 30966

E-mail: hotrodlarkin@aol.com
Phone: (404) 555-1029

> There is joy in work... There is no happiness except in the
> realization that we have accomplished something.
> - Henry Ford

April 19, 1999

Notice quote to open the letter, as well as intermittent headlines to separate themes and convey key points. This letter is structured more like a business marketing letter than a conventional "job search" letter.

Mr. Harold Crane, Sales Manager
Tri-County Lincoln-Mercury
1700 North Main Street
Atlanta, GA 30951

Dear Mr. Crane:

I am preparing to graduate Copper College with a Bachelor's in Automotive Management in May of this year and am seeking an entry-level position in the automotive field, specifically with Tri-County Lincoln-Mercury. I have enclosed my resume for your consideration.

Tri-County Lincoln-Mercury - Where Quality is Job One !

I enjoy the history of the automotive industry and Henry Ford is certainly a person we can all learn from. The quote above means a lot to me because I want to enjoy my work, and know that success and rewards stem directly from achievement. Tri-County Lincoln-Mercury is a recognized leader in the Atlanta market and I am impressed with the service and quality awards you have won over the past 12 years, especially "Dealer of the Decade." I have not only witnessed your impressive growth and expansion over the past 10 years, but my family *has purchased two vehicles from you* and know first-hand that quality and personalized service are your trademarks ! I would like to be a contributing member of your team and work hard toward achieving your organizational and sales goals and objectives.

I Will Pay My Dues and Meet Your High Standards For Success Achievement

I love the automotive industry and feel comfortable in sales, administration, or customer service. I have strong technical skills, an in-depth knowledge of automotive products - especially Ford and Lincoln-Mercury brands - and have solid salesmanship skills to maximize sales and service efforts for both new or used vehicles - automobiles or trucks.

May We Get Together and Discuss Next Steps?

If you believe, as I do, that my qualifications and experience would greatly contribute to your organizational goals and objectives, I would welcome the opportunity to introduce myself and my credentials to you in a personal interview to further evaluate if an employment opportunity might be mutually beneficial. Please expect my telephone call in the coming week to arrange such a meeting or you may call me anytime on my cellular phone (555-2468).

Thank you for your time and consideration. I look forward to meeting/speaking with you soon.

Sincerely,

Donald P. Larkin

Encl.: Resume

DONALD R. CALVIN
2727 Green Way
Loretto, PA 15940   (814) 555-2233

> "Donald is the finest Journeyman Carpenter I have had the pleasure of working with in more than 30 years."
>
> *Terrel Murphy, Master Carpenter, Lic. #5239654*

August 18, 1999

Mr. Michael Cordner
Cordner Construction and Renovation Corp.
2300 South Park Drive
Pittsburgh, PA 16678

Quote to open lends much credibility.

Dear Mr. Cordner:

I am exploring employment opportunities as **Lead Carpenter** with your company. I have enclosed my resume for your review.

I am a young, energetic, quality-oriented professional who takes pride in my work. As you can see from the quotation above, I strive very hard to be the very best carpenter - ensuring quality craftsmanship consistent with customer expectations and demands.

Cordner Construction and Renovation Corp. is considered the #1 contractor in the Pittsburgh area - a company who has the reputation for employing the very best tradesmen. I would like to become a contributing member of your quality team.

I would like to meet with you personally to introduce myself and determine if there might be a possible fit with your company. I will take the liberty of calling you next week to arrange such a meeting. Thank you for your time and consideration.

Respectfully,

Donald R. Calvin

SUSAN G. KILGORE
2255 Carriage Way
San Francisco, CA 94109
(415) 555-2468 / Imageconsultant@aol.com

> **Susan is one of the top Certified Image Consultants I have come in contact with. She has a keen sense for understanding national and international markets and positioning corporate image to meet corporate operational, marketing, and customer service goals and objectives.**
>
> *-Glenn F. Hall, Executive V.P. Compaq Computers, Inc.*

April 27, 1999

Quote to open lends much credibility. Centered headlines convey key message points.

Mr. Wayne G. Graham, President
Global Software, Ltd.
18 Bragan Boulevard
San Francisco, CA 94220

Dear Mr. Graham:

Cynthia Wilcox referred me to you and mentioned that you are considering contracting with/hiring an image consultant to help launch your new retail software program (ACCOUNT-LINE) internationally. The project sounds exciting to me, especially since I have recently concluded a highly successful two-year assignment with Compaq Computers in the international arena.

Key Contacts Presently in Place

I read with interest Global Software's Annual Report that was distributed in February and noticed that you plan to target and infiltrate the European Market beginning this summer - with plans to expand into Asia in the year 2000. I believe that through strong marketing and image building, Global Software can capture significant marketshare in less than 12 months as a result of my key network of contacts.

Partnering With Global - A Flexible Approach

I am highly flexible in how I can best serve Global's interest and needs - as a full-time employee, a full or part time consultant, or on an assignment to assignment basis. I am a professional who believes in "measurable results," and have a program that I am confident will impress you with quantifiable measures of success !

5-to-1 Return on Investment !

Over the past 12 years, I have worked with/for 18 Fortune 500 companies and dozens of small to medium sized organizations. I am proud of my track record of being able to verifiably show a five-to-one return on the image consulting investment. I developed a "maintenance program" for Compaq Computer where they are now able to achieve impressive growth and expansion results for a fraction on the $210,000. I can do the same for your new product (ACCOUNT-LINE).

Next Steps - Schedule an Introductory Meeting

I would like to introduce myself and more of my ideas to you personally and will plan to telephone you early next week. I have enclosed my resume, portfolio of past projects, and testimonials letters from key executives supporting my past accomplishments and achievements. Hopefully this will be helpful in further introducing my skills and qualifications. I thank you for your time and consideration and look forward to speaking with you next week.

Sincerely,

Susan G. Kilgore
Certified Image Consultant

ROBERT C. LEEMAN

1800 West Abbey Road, New York, NY 10023
Home: (201) 555-7345 / Fax: (201) 555-9812
E-mail: Stockmkt35@aol.com

> ***"Rule #1: Never Lose Money. Rule #2: Never Forget Rule #1"***
> *- Warren Buffet*

March 18, 1999

Mr. Joel Lansing Jr., Vice President
Salomon Smith Barney
120 Wall Street, Suite 800
New York, NY 10021

Interesting attention-grabbing quotation. Boxed section headers also create a clean, easy-to-read look while maintaining much "punch."

Dear Joel:

Thank you for spending 90 minutes of your time with me last Thursday. I am very serious about joining the Salomon Smith Barney family and servicing and expanding my client base with your fine organization. As we discussed last week, I have three basic philosophical beliefs that have made me successful and that I believe are congruent with the business philosophy of Salomon Smith Barney. I would like to reiterate my position at this time.

Investment Philosophy

- There is no substitute for knowledge - investing is a head game, knowing the difference between price and value
- Avoid risk, don't gamble, and seek out opportunity - think long term
- Adopt the right tools, build a circle of competence (surround yourself with the best), and sell only what you understand

Customer Service Philosophy

- Act with the client's best interests in mind
- Communicate well; educate and motivate clients to be active participants in the investment process
- Always do what's right - set the example

Philosophy of Integrity

- Be honest
- Cultivate good character
- Reputation is everything

I am prepared to make a career decision within the next 60 days. I will be available to meet with Joseph Delecruz the week of the 6th as you proposed. I will contact you in the coming week to lock in a date and time. Until then, I again thank you for your interest in me, and I eagerly anticipate our next round of discussions. Have a great week !

Sincerely,

Robert C. Leeman

BETTY JEAN ST. CLAIRE

18 Rose Garden Terrace
Edwardsville, IL 62003
(618) 555-2565 / Bookworm2000@aol.com

> *I don't think much of a man who is not wiser today than he was yesterday.*
> **- Abraham Lincoln**

July 18, 1999

Mrs. Janine Hiller, Head Librarian
Southern Illinois University
100 University Drive
Edwardsville, IL 60611

> *Like all letters in this section, the opening headline is a strong attention grabber. The section headers make the letter easier to read and understand.*

Dear Mrs. Hiller:

I am respectfully responding to your advertisement in the <u>Sunday Journal</u> for position as Head Research Librarian. I have enclosed my resume for your review.

QUALIFICATIONS

I believe the most effective way for showcasing my potential value to your institution would be to highlight my qualifications:

Chairperson:	City of Chicago Library Board Member, 1992 - Present
Delegate:	To the Illinois Governor's Conference on Library and Information Services, 1998
Delegate:	To the White House Conferences on Library and Information Services, 1993
Librarian:	Seven years experience as Research Librarian, Duncan High School, Chicago IL, 1968-75
Media Services:	Recipient: *Outstanding Media Services Award*, ITA Association, 1975, 1976, 1977, 1978

INTERNET RESEARCH

In addition to solid experience in library and media services, I have developed an award-winning research program (elementary - high school students) for using the Internet as a research tool - a pilot program that was so successful, that it is now in use in nearly 100% of the Illinois high schools. I believe I can adapt this program to meet the needs of college and post-graduate students as well.

CONTRIBUTIONS TO SOUTHERN ILLINOIS UNIVERSITY

I retired as Principal and would like to complete my career in academia as a Librarian with your institution. I offer you five key strengths in addition to the vast experience in this arena:

* High Energy   *** Passion For Learning**   *** Passion For Teaching**   *** Integrity**   *** Reputation**

If you feel my qualifications can contribute to your future growth, I would be interested in meeting with you to discuss how we can team up and achieve challenging goals and objectives. Thank you for your time and consideration.

Sincerely,

Betty Jean St. Claire

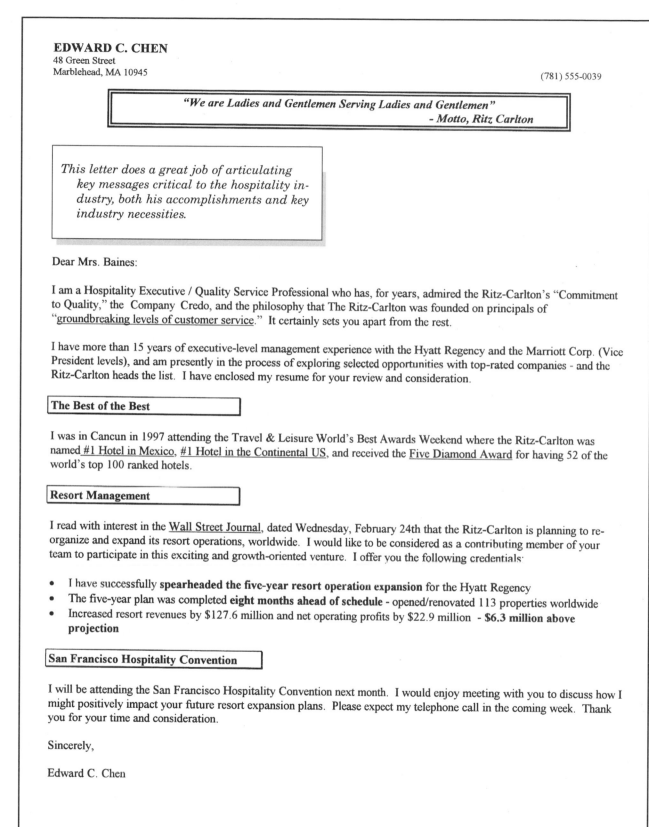

EDWARD C. CHEN
48 Green Street
Marblehead, MA 10945

(781) 555-0039

> *"We are Ladies and Gentlemen Serving Ladies and Gentlemen"*
> *- Motto, Ritz Carlton*

This letter does a great job of articulating key messages critical to the hospitality industry, both his accomplishments and key industry necessities.

Dear Mrs. Baines:

I am a Hospitality Executive / Quality Service Professional who has, for years, admired the Ritz-Carlton's "Commitment to Quality," the Company Credo, and the philosophy that The Ritz-Carlton was founded on principals of "groundbreaking levels of customer service." It certainly sets you apart from the rest.

I have more than 15 years of executive-level management experience with the Hyatt Regency and the Marriott Corp. (Vice President levels), and am presently in the process of exploring selected opportunities with top-rated companies - and the Ritz-Carlton heads the list. I have enclosed my resume for your review and consideration.

The Best of the Best

I was in Cancun in 1997 attending the Travel & Leisure World's Best Awards Weekend where the Ritz-Carlton was named #1 Hotel in Mexico, #1 Hotel in the Continental US, and received the Five Diamond Award for having 52 of the world's top 100 ranked hotels.

Resort Management

I read with interest in the Wall Street Journal, dated Wednesday, February 24th that the Ritz-Carlton is planning to re-organize and expand its resort operations, worldwide. I would like to be considered as a contributing member of your team to participate in this exciting and growth-oriented venture. I offer you the following credentials·

- I have successfully **spearheaded the five-year resort operation expansion** for the Hyatt Regency
- The five-year plan was completed **eight months ahead of schedule** - opened/renovated 113 properties worldwide
- Increased resort revenues by $127.6 million and net operating profits by $22.9 million - **$6.3 million above projection**

San Francisco Hospitality Convention

I will be attending the San Francisco Hospitality Convention next month. I would enjoy meeting with you to discuss how I might positively impact your future resort expansion plans. Please expect my telephone call in the coming week. Thank you for your time and consideration.

Sincerely,

Edward C. Chen

WARREN H. DIAMOND

A Diamond is a "Company's" Best Friend

May 9, 1999

Mr. Tyron Ross / National Sales Manager
B&L Leather Furniture, Inc.
8200 Main Street
Rochester, NY 12321

Headline with candidate's last name is a bit bold, but is striking. Table does a good job of demonstrating sales accomplishments and salary growth.

Dear Mr. Ross:

I noticed you advertisement in the <u>Rochester News</u> for the position of Lead salesman. I have enclosed my resume of qualifications for your consideration.

You requested, in your advertisement, a salary history to accompany the cover letter and resume. Actually, I feel that I can best highlight my potential value to your organization in terms of past production and performance. I have been working for DB Brown and Company since 1993 and provide you with my five-year track record:

Year	# of Clients	Total Sales	Lost Accounts	Service Levels	Salary/Bonuses
1993	187	325,000	0	99.4%	78,000
1994	209	399,000	0	99.5%	84,000
1995	228	437,000	0	99.6%	92,000
1996	267	518,000	0	99.5%	102,000
1997	312	712,000	0	99.6%	115,000
1998	409	902,000	0	99.6%	138,000

As you can see, a Diamond (Warren Diamond) can be a "company's" best friend. I attribute my success to three key elements:

1) **Discipline and hard work**
2) **Strong networking and relationship-building skills**
3) **Attention to detail - never letting anything "slip through the cracks"**

If you feel my qualifications and past accomplishments are indicative of what I might be able to do for your company, I would welcome the opportunity of discussing potential employment possibilities. Feel free to contact me at your earliest convenience to arrange for a personal interview. Thank you for your time and consideration.

Sincerely,

Warren H. Diamond

HERNANDO F. CORTEZ

1818 Southwest 8th Avenue, PH-2
Miami, FL 33385
Home: (305) 555-7395 / Mobile: (305) 555-0009

---
2 + 2 = $18.2 billion

January 26, 1999

Mr. Arthur Cross, Vice President / National Sales Manager
Williamson & Cross Telecommunications, Ltd.
92000 State Road Seven
Miami, FL 33365

> *Mathematical headline provokes interest to read on. Strong, themed letter.*

Dear Mr. Cross:

I have been closely following Williamson & Cross for the past three years and have been extremely impressed with the growth of your organization. In particular, I have been impressed with the aggressive approach you have taken to opening new and emerging markets in Central and South America - the most recent public report indicating that you have increased sales in this region 389% or $24.7 million over the past 15 months alone!

17 Years Telecommunications Expertise

I have been in the telecommunications industry for the past 17 years with internationally recognized firms. In the past 10 years, I have spent <u>60% of my time doing business in Central and South America</u> (with side trips to Europe and the Pacific Rim countries). I have a regional reputation as a **Top Sales Producer** and am proud to say that I have never lost an account to a competitor.

How does 2+2 = $18.2 billion? Making Math Work For Williamson & Cross

Accurate market assessment, key contact development, and strong presentation, negotiating, and closing skills have been my trademarks for the past 17 years. I have closed over $289 million of business in that time and have helped two companies go public as a result of this unprecedented growth.

Here's how 2+2 = $18.2 billion. I identified the two key decision makers in both Venezuela and Brazil (two countries and two decision makers in each country). I discovered what their chief concern was, identified concrete methods of saving them millions and millions of dollars, and demonstrated that over the long term, service and maintenance costs would be minimal. The result was nothing less than amazing - $18.2 <u>billion</u> worth of business over the next 20 years. I am confident that I can ignite business for Williamson & Cross as well.

Next Steps

I will be returning from Colombia the 23rd of February and will be in the Miami area for three weeks before I fly back to Mexico and then on to South America. I would like to propose a two-hour lunch on Wednesday the 25th of February to discuss possible employment opportunities and to present you with a comprehensive outline of how I feel I can benefit Williamson & Cross.

Though I am relatively happy with my current employer, there are internal changes that will significantly impact the company's ability to do business in Central and South America. I eagerly anticipate our meeting in February.

Sincerely,

Hernando F. Cortez

JSR, Inc.
Seminars International

> *Jerry is one of the finest Seminar Facilitators I have ever met. He is a high-energy, high-impact communicator who delivers his messages in an effective and entertaining fashion. He consistently receives top ratings from small community groups to Fortune 500 companies.*
>
> **- Stephen R. Covey**

June 8, 1999

Opening reference is always strong, especially from someone recognizable like Stephen Covey.

Mr. Bud Hollings, President
Hollings Entertainment Services, Inc.
802 West Hollywood Boulevard
Los Angeles, 97662

Dear Mr. Hollings:

I had the opportunity to work with world renown author, speaker, and coach Dr. Stephen R. Covey as a contracted seminar leader and workshop facilitator over the past 4 years. Dr. Covey suggested I contact you to promote and facilitate his programs as well as others for your organization. I have enclosed my resume and video presentation for your review and consideration.

Synopsis of my work history

♦ Between 1988 and 1994 I worked for CareerTrac - as a seminar leader in the areas of Time Management, Stress Management, Change Management, and Goal Setting and Long and Short Term Strategic Planning.

♦ I was recruited by the Covey Organization in 1995 to facilitate their three main programs: Organizational Leadership, Growth Management & Development, and Value-Oriented Living. I was a subcontractor for the Covey Organization (75%) as well as for CareerTrac (25%).

International capabilities

I have enjoyed these past 11+ years but feel that I must expand my curriculum and your organization is recognized for its plethora of seminars and workshops that you present internationally. I speak fluent French and Spanish, and feel I can be an asset to your company both here in the US as well as abroad (or within the US with foreign clientele).

Awards and recognitions

Covey National Recognition Award for Presentation Excellence, 1996, 1997, 1998
NSA Platinum Award, 1998
NSA Gold Award, 1997

Please expect my telephone call in the coming week to arrange such a meeting or you may call me at anytime at the number noted above. Thank you for your time and consideration. I look forward to meeting/speaking with you soon.

Sincerely,

Jerry S. Robertson

RACHAEL H. WHITTIER

99 Reddingstone Drive, West
Montreal, Canada H5P-8T3
Home: (514) 555-5668 / Fax: (514) 555-1123

E-mail: Skibum101@mailnet.net   Website: www.skibum101.com

> *"I will always be someone who wants to do it better than others.   I love competition."*
> **- Jean-Claude Killy**

July 20, 1999

Mr. Harold Goodel, Head Coach
US Ski Team
200 Olympic Way
Aspen, CO 47336

> *Quotation is a good attention grabber, and the section headers break up the letter and make it more interesting to read. Remember, appearance is critical at this juncture.*

Dear Mr. Goodel:

I believe Audrey King mentioned that I would be writing to you regarding a position as Assistant Olympic Downhill Ski Instructor for the US Olympic Team. I have enclosed my summary of qualifications for your review in hopes of becoming a contributing member of your team - in pursuit of Olympic Gold Medals in the upcoming Winter Olympics.

The Killy Philosophy

In competition, I know there is only one goal - to be the best! I was coached in this philosophy and have coached downhill champions using it as well.   I have coached two Canadian Downhill Champions over the past six years and am now interested in utilizing my successful coaching techniques in assisting the US Olympic Ski Team achieve Olympic success in the next Winter Olympic Games.

No Defection—Just Marriage!

As Audrey may have told you, I was recently married to an American and will be applying for American Citizenship. In the meantime, I am a Permanent Resident of the U.S. and have moved from Montreal to Aspen. I am presently a ski instructor at Snow Mass during the winter months and am a personal trainer and physical therapist during the summer season. I would love to be able to utilize my strong teaching and coaching skills in helping the American Olympic Team achieve success in downhill skiing.

Let's Rendezvous and Discuss Next Steps!

I understand you will be in Aspen the third week of August. I would welcome the opportunity to meet with you, introduce myself and my coaching philosophy/techniques, and determine how I might be a contributing member of your instructional team. I have enclosed a 12 minute video on my past skiing accomplishments, both as a skier as well as a coach. I will contact your office later next week to solidify a time and place to meet that is convenient for you.

Thank you for your consideration and I look forward to meeting with you next month.

Sincerely,

Rachael H. Whittier

11

Cover Letters and the Internet

If you are sending an electronic or e-mailed resume, your e-mail will open with a note. This is your new cover letter. The differences in a cover letter sent online are probably more pronounced than the change in your resume. e-mailed cover letters should be considered short introductions, not nearly as long as what you might write out and put in the mail.

Your e-mailed cover letter might also be used as a source of keywords for computer searches. It should include at least a few keywords (nouns) that will give the reader an overview of your qualifications.

The same general principles of a cover letter apply to an e-mailed one. However, it is critical to keep it short and maintain the same formatting guidelines assumed for the electronic resume. This means that you need to choose a monotype font (one equally spaced for each letter) so the spacing won't get lost in the data transport. When you e-mail a note, the networks transport it in ASCII format, which means it is converted into a generic format and loses formatting such as underlining, bold typeface, italics, and creative font choices. ASCII only converts spacing and tabs, but no other formatting.

Finally, the key parts listed in Chapter 5, Anatomy of a Cover Letter, won't apply here because when you e-mail a letter, the headings and address formats are embedded in the e-mail itself. The style will vary, as illustrated by the following examples.

So, keep your e-mail letter short and simple, but make sure it still contains enough punch to generate interest in you.

25 TIPS FOR USING THE INTERNET IN YOUR JOB SEARCH

1. When typing your resume out with the intent of e-mailing, make sure it is in ASCII format (see page 97)

2. Use keywords (see page 189) heavily in the introduction of the resume, not at the end.

3. Keywords are almost always nouns related to skills, such as financial analysis, marketing, accounting, Web design.

4. When sending your resume via e-mail in ASCII format, attach (if you can) a nicely formatted version in case the ASCII version does go through and the reader would like to see your creativity and preferred layout. If you do attach a formatted version, use a common program like MS Word.

5. Don't focus on an objective in the introduction of the resume but rather on accomplishments, using keywords to describe them.

6. Don't post your resume to your own Web site unless it is a very slick page. A poorly executed Web page is more damaging than none at all.

7. Before you e-mail your resume, experiment by sending it to yourself and to a friend as a test drive.

8. Look up the Web site of the company you are targeting to get recent information about new products, etc. and look at their job posting for new information.

9. Before your interview or verbal contact, research the company's Web site.

10. Use a font size between 10 and 14 points, make it all the same for an ASCII format resume, and don't create your resume for e-mailing with lines exceeding 65 characters.

11. In case your resume will be scanned, use white paper with no borders and no creative fonts.

12. Include your e-mail address on your resume and cover letter.

13. Don't e-mail your resume from your current employer's network.

14. Don't circulate your work e-mail address for job search purposes.

15. In the "subject" of your e-mail (just below the "address to" section), put something more creative than "Resume Enclosed." Try "Resume showing 8 years in telecommunications industry," for example.

16. For additional sources of on-line job searching, do a "search" on the Web for job searching, your targeted company, and your specific discipline for additional information.

17. Be careful of your spelling on the Net. You will notice more spelling errors on e-mail exchanges than you will ever see in mailed letter exchanges.

18. Try to make sure your resume is scannable. This means it uses a simple font, has no borders, no creative lining, no boldface, no underlining, no italics and limited or no columning. Though the practice of scanning is overestimated, it should still be a consideration.

19. Purchase or check out of a library an Internet directory listing the many links to job opportunities out there. There are thousands.

20. If you are using e-mail for your cover letter, keep it brief. If the reader is reading on-screen, the tolerance for reading long passages of information is reduced dramatically.

21. Always back up what you can on a disk.

22. If you post your resume to a newsgroup, make sure that is acceptable to avoid any problems with other participants.

23. Remember that tabs and spaces are the only formatting you can use in ASCII files.

24. Make sure you check your e-mail every day. If you are communicating via the Net, people expect a prompt return.

25. Don't send multiple e-mails to insure one gets through. Try to send it with a confirmation of receipt, or keep a lookout for a notice from your ISP that the message didn't go through.

> *Letter is brief, very important for E-mailed letters. E-mailed letters don't require the structure of traditional letters, other than the body of letter.*

To:advertisingjobs.net;jobsearch.net;employment.com;engineeringnetworking.com
Date: May 14, 1998
Subject: Seeking advertising account executive position

I am interested in finding a position with a Big 6 advertising firm in the capacity of advertising account executive. I have worked in advertising for 3 years, and past accounts include Procter and Gamble, Dave and Busters, Cisco and Ethan Allen.

I am the lead account manager for Dave and Busters and Cisco. Duties include contract negotiation, liaison between client and creative and oversee creative development.

Please see attached resume if you are interested. If you know of any relevant contacts, please forward leads to me, or feel free to forward this email and the attached resume. I really appreciate it!

Sincerely,

Sharon Elessee
selessee@sprintmail.com   Attachment: [resume.doc]

11-2

This is a newsgroup posting for networking on the net. Letter is brief and to the point, not wordy or full of "fluff."

To: jobsearch.net;employment.com;engineeringnetworking.com
Date: October 2, 1999
Subject: Seeking radio frequency (RF) engineering position

I am interested in networking through this group to find a RF engineering position in either Denver or Phoenix with a cellular or PCS wireless organization.

I have worked with AT&T Wireless services in their TDMA deployment in two new PCS markets (Chicago and Milwaukee). I am very skilled with the latest forecasting tools and optimization methods for both TDMA and CDMA platforms. Attached is my resume for those interested. My references and work history are both very solid. Any tips or suggestions you may have are welcomed.

Thanks !

David Brodsky
david.brodsky@worldnet.net   Attachment: [resume.doc]

11-3

This letter is a follow-up to an interview / meeting. Closure includes pertinent information at the bottom but is properly absent of formatting.

Dear Mr. Smith:

I really enjoyed meeting with you yesterday. It was interesting hearing all of Blockbuster's exciting new plans, and I was particularly excited about how this position fits into the big picture.

My skills would be a real advantage for Blockbuster at this time. I relish opportunities to be creative and solve problems, and it was great to see that Blockbuster hasn't lost its innovative spirit as it's grown. I agree you need someone who is flexible and comfortable working under pressure and time constraints, and I believe my skill set and mind set are a good match.

I'm sure many of the candidates you interviewed have the technical skills to function as a Field Support Representative. You stressed the importance of decision making in this position. That is one aspect that may distinguish me. I believe in problem solving and making decisions, and showing my supervisor the desired end result, not a half-finished product. Please follow up with my previous employer as we discussed.

I hope to hear from you soon. If you have any questions please call me at home.

Sincerely,

Roberta Alexander
ra@att.net
222 Highway 18, Scarsdale, NY 10001
(914) 555-8699

11-4

Dear Ms. Goff:

My experience in business management and marketing is an excellent fit for your new telecommunications start up in Southern California. I have watched Cox with much envy as you launched your PCS network in other markets, and wanted to take this opportunity to introduce myself.

Though I did not see a market development opening on your web site, I am confident that I am a good fit and would like to be available for consideration should a good fit come along.

Though I am currently employed, I am very interested in Cox, and would like the opportunity to discuss your future market developments.

Sincerely,

Beth Pasterz
bpasterz@airmail.net
3255 Phillips Street
San Juan Capistrano, CA 90299
(714) 555-5687

Notice that the formatting structure is simple and lacks complicated designs that could be distorted while sent over the Net.

Dear Ms. Lane:

Please allow me to introduce myself. I am new to the Michigan area. I have worked in the chemical products industry for the last six years, and am interested in continuing in that industry here. I had spent the last seven years in Chicago, but a recent engagement has brought me to central Michigan.

I worked for ABC Chemical in Chicago, moved on to XYZ Chemical for 2 years, and have received promotions en route with each company. Considering Dow is such a prominent player in the industry, I feel lucky to have been moved here.

My background lies in product development within the industry. I was on the market launch team that rolled out synthetic covering for wet weather shields. We gained a 17% share within 18 months of our launch, very strong by XYZ standards.

I will stop by your office next Tuesday between 2PM and 3PM to fill out your formal application. If you can take a few moments to see me at that time, I would be very grateful. I will call you on Monday to see if this can be arranged.

Thank you for your attention. I am excited about the possibility of joining Dow Chemical Company.

Sincerely,

Mary Beth Rouse
mbr@aol.com
4799 E. Deckerville Road
Saginaw, MI 48569 (517) 555-5682

12
Networking Cover Letters

One career design technique that is widely recognized as *the* most effective technique in securing employment opportunities is networking, the process of engaging your network of family, friends, and associates to help you identify and obtain the job you desire. The networking cover letter is a letter communicating to your network of contacts that you are seeking employment. The letter clearly defines your skills, what types of opportunities you are seeking, and specific organizations you'd like to work for. It is still true, like it or not, that it is not so much what you know that counts, but who you know. An effectively written networking letter will help you to 1) take full advantage of your network of contacts or 2) begin developing and improving a network to expand your influence.

We offer several examples of how to write a networking cover letter, and 25 additional tips on networking.

25 NETWORKING TIPS

1. Two-thirds of all jobs are secured via the networking process. Networking is a systematic approach to cultivating formal and informal contacts for the purpose of gaining information, enhancing visibility in the market, and obtaining referrals.

2. Effective networking requires self-confidence, poise, and personal conviction.

3. You must first know the companies and organizations you wish to work for. That will determine the type of network you will develop and nurture.

4. Focus on meeting the "right people." This takes planning and preparation.

5. Target close friends, family members, neighbors, social acquaintances, social and religious group members, business contacts, teachers, and community leaders.

6. Include employment professionals as an important part of your network. This includes headhunters and personnel agency executives. They have a wealth of knowledge about job and market conditions.

7. Remember, networking is a numbers game. Once you have a network of people in place, prioritize the listing so you have separated top priority contacts from lower priority ones.

8. Sometimes you may have to pay for advice and information. Paying consultants or professionals or investing in Internet services is part of the job search process today, as long as it's legal and ethical.

9. Know what you want from your contacts. If you don't know what you want, neither will your network of people. Specific questions will get specific answers.

10. Ask for advice, not for a job. You cannot contact someone asking if they know of any job openings. The answer will invariably be no, especially at higher levels. You need to ask for things like industry advice, advice on geographic areas, etc. The job insights will follow but will be almost incidental. This positioning will build value for you and make the contact person more comfortable about helping you.

11. Watch your attitude and demeanor at all times. Everyone you come in contact with is a potential member of your network. Demonstrate enthusiasm and professionalism at all times.

12. Keep a file on each member of your network and maintain good records at all times. A well-organized network filing system or database will yield superior results.

13. Get comfortable on the telephone. Good telephone communication skills are critical.

14. Travel the "information highway." Networking is more effective if you have E-mail, fax, and computer capabilities.

15. Be well prepared for your conversation, whether in person or over the phone. You should have a script in your mind of how to answer questions, what to ask, and what you're trying to accomplish.

16. Do not fear rejection. If a contact cannot help you, move on to the next contact. Do not take rejection personally—it's just part of the process.

17. Flatter the people in your network. It's been said that the only two types of people who can be flattered are men and women. Use tact, courtesy, and flattery.

18. If a person in your network cannot personally help, advise, or direct you, ask for referrals.

19. Keep in touch with the major contacts in your network on a monthly basis. Remember, out of sight, out of mind.

20. Don't abuse the networking process. Networking is a two-way street. Be honest and brief and offer your contacts something in return for their time, advice, and information. This can be as simple as a lunch or offering your professional services in return for their cooperation.

21. Show an interest in your contacts. Cavette Robert, one of the founders of the National Speakers Association, said, "People don't care how much you

know, until they know how much you care." Show how much you care. It will get you anywhere.

22. Send thank-you notes following each networking contact.

23. Seek out key networking contacts in professional and trade associations.

24. Carry calling cards with you at all times to hand out to anyone and everyone you come in contact with. Include your name, address, phone number, areas of expertise, and specific skill areas.

25. Socialize and get out more than ever before. Networking requires dedication and massive amounts of energy. Consistently work on expanding your network.

Debbie McMullen
1215 Phillips Drive
New York, NY 10001
(212) 555-9555

December 3, 1998

Ms. Beth Pasterz
Robert Half International
1222 Park Avenue
New York, NY 10012

Dear Ms. Pasterz:

Thanks for speaking with me on the phone earlier. I agree that there probably isn't a good match between me and your current positions to fill. However, you did mention that based on our phone interview you thought my credentials were strong, and it got me thinking.

Would you mind if we still met? I am new to the New York area as my husband was just transferred, and it looks like we'll be here for quite a while. You seemed to be fairly well connected and in the know as to what's going on here. I would love to meet just to get your advice on which firms I might avoid, which might be good, and what the overall climate is like in New York.

I realize you are probably quite busy, and I'd be happy to buy you breakfast or lunch just to talk for a few minutes. I promise I won't monopolize your time. You never know, maybe I will be calling you soon to help me recruit my new accounting staff.

I will call you on Friday and try to set something up. Thanks, I really enjoyed talking with you today.

Best Regards,

Debbie McMullen

Opening reference to a former meeting builds instant bridge with reader. Asking for advice will almost always receive a positive response.

Melanie Jordan

March 12, 1999

Ms. Alicia Paramo
Group Accounting Manager, Arthur Anderson
201 Akard Street, Suite 4200
Dallas, TX 75001

Dear Ms. Paramo:

I don't know if you will remember, but we met when your firm was doing some auditing work for Texas Oil. I was performing some legal work, as I am an attorney specializing in environmental law. I was very impressed with you and your team, and have a small favor to ask.

I have been with my firm for some time, and am interested in leaving in favor of a smaller firm. You seemed to know a lot about the industry as well as who's who in Dallas, and I'd like to ask your advice on the business climate here.

I will call you next week to try to set something up, and would love to take you to lunch or dinner to talk a little shop. I'd really appreciate any time you can offer.

Thanks, and I look forward to talking with you next week!

Best Regards,

Melanie Jordan

DAN ARTHUR ◆ 1314 LOS COLINAS BLVD. APT. 114A ◆ IRVING, TEXAS 75033

September 12, 1998

This letter provides the reader with a good overview of what he is looking for and what his qualifications are. This is a good example of writing a good networking letter to a friend.

Mr. Ron Sanders
2818 Bradford Street
San Antonio, TX 78213

Hey Ron,

Greetings from North Texas! As usual, I'm keeping my options open when it comes to job opportunities so I thought I would check on the employment market there in San Antonio. I know you have a lot of contacts with the local VM SHARE organization and there are still plenty of companies that use the old mainframes (they're calling them Enterprise Servers now).

This new perspective fits right in with my new job interests. You know I've always been interested in networking computers. I was into the Internet before it was the Internet—when it was ArpaNet and MilNet back in the late 'eighties. When we were contractors at Kelly Air Force Base, I caught the networking bug working with the Defense Data Network.

I still have a soft spot for the "care and feeding" of large mainframes and I keep my hand in with the new OS/390 operating system, and of course with VTAM and CICS. That fits right in my new bag of tricks which includes my ability to network just about every platform you know about with anything else. I'm using servers, bridges, routers, UNIX, AIX, Windows/NT, IBM ComManager, SNA, TCP/IP, LANs, WANs (Frame Relay included), satellite links and even Datalink Control Switching.

Ten, even five years ago we never realized there were so many ways to connect two, or ten, or even a hundred computers together. The thought of moving gigabytes of data between them in a few minutes was mind-boggling. Now I work in that environment every day. Who'da thought?

So—how about checking with our old buddies over at USAA and Hart-Hanks to see if they can use an old dog who's learned a bunch of new tricks. I'm enclosing a few copies of my current resume to pass around. Call me in the evening at 972.555.4819 or Email me at DArthur@aol.com if you have any hot news.

Thanks! All my best to Nikki.

Your friend,

Dan

Enclosure

Michael Peters

613 Yellow Rose Lane, Plano, TX 75892 (972) 555-5893

May 14, 1998

> *Real point of this letter is to demonstrate that Michael understands the needs of today's businesses, and that he would make a good person to refer or help network.*

Mr. Dennis Dudash
846 Blue Ridge Circle
Addison, TX 75241

Dear Denny:

How is everything? I appreciate your offer to introduce me to some people as I begin exploring other career opportunities. My work at Suntel has been rewarding, but I think it is time to move on, as we discussed last week.

With Suntel, I have been able to really develop skills that would be useful to many other companies. Research we conducted identified key business drivers common to all businesses: they have trouble hiring and keeping good employees; they need to develop products that better meet their customer needs; they need to get new products to market quicker.

My background in market development honed my skills in developing products and matching them with target segments very effectively. Our most recent line of demoflatchees achieved a 17% share in only six months! That kind of market presence should be valuable to many companies.

I have attached a few resumes for your reference and distribution to any key contacts you may know. Thanks in advance for all your help. I owe you a nice Texas steak dinner for this one!

Sincerely,

Michael Peters

Phillip Jackson

1032 Old County Road, St. Petersburg, Florida 33702
814-555-5678   e-mail pjackson@ibm.net

August 10, 1998

James Hawthorne
Megamanufacturer, Inc.
8507 Mega Square West
Cincinnati, OH 45212

Good opening by asking for advice, not a job. Also provides the reader with relevant background on the networker.

Dear Jim:

May I ask your advice and assistance?

As you know, for the last eight years I've been continuously challenged with new marketing assignments for Superskin and I've delivered impressive sales and profit gains for all of the brands I've managed. However, now that Tracy has begun serious gymnastics training at Cincinnati Gymnastics Academy, Wendy and I would prefer to relocate to your area to minimize the separation.

Jim, since you know my abilities and potential to contribute, would you take a moment to think about people I can contact at large manufacturing/consumer goods businesses in the Cincinnati area? I'm confident that I can bring to my next employer the same strong results I delivered for Superskin:

- Improved both sales and profits for several of the company's signature brands (Superskin skin creams, Ladyfair makeup, and BabySkin).
- As Brand Manager for the entire BabySkin brand, led the brand's first sales growth since its acquisition 10 years ago.
- Led the turnaround of Ladyfair's teen products, increasing sales 15% and profits $22 million.

In addition to any contacts you can suggest, I would greatly appreciate your insight with regard to the Cincinnati job market. To assist you in evaluating appropriate contacts and suggestions, I have enclosed a resume and offer the following important elements for my next position:

- Leadership of a large-scale marketing initiative, preferably in the consumer goods industry.
- The opportunity to have a significant, positive impact on the organization and its growth and direction.
- Focus on overall market strategy as opposed to "quick fixes" (though I certainly have the background to pull these off and would be glad to offer my insight to a company facing such a challenge).
- An organization that values its resources, especially people.

Thanks, Jim. I look forward to hearing your suggestions. I will follow up with a phone call to your office next week and I hope I can take you to lunch on my next visit to Cincinnati.

Sincerely,

Phillip Jackson

enclosure

NIKA NIKSIRAT
215 Hartman Drive
Portsmouth, NH 03801
(603) 555-4606

June 2, 1999

Introduction builds instant rapport with reader. She stresses she is looking for advice, not a job. That will help her get the meeting she wants.

Mr. Benjamin Chang
Technical Director, Cisco Systems
4399 Central Avenue
Boston, MA 18002

Dear Mr. Chang:

Dave Tinker from Cellcorp suggested I contact you. He said that you "know more about the network router business than anyone this side of the Mason-Dixon line." I knew you would be someone I had to meet.

Though I am employed with Bell Atlantic, I have decided to make a career move toward a more entrepreneurial start-up operation. I am not writing you for a position, but rather wanted to get some industry advice from you. Companies that are just starting out are usually well capitalized (like Level 3) but may be short on technical or operational expertise.

Having been involved with several major product launches with Bell Atlantic, I feel I have been through it all. However, going forward I think I can make a greater impact with a start-up. A start-up will be able to utilize my experience, and it could be a good situation for them and me.

I will call you next week to talk to you for a few minutes. Don't worry, I only want some advice, and if you have the time, I would love to take you to lunch. Thanks in advance for all your time!

Sincerely,

Nika Niksirat

13

Referral Cover Letters

When you have your network of contacts in place, one of your strategies will be to ask for and work on personal and professional referrals. A referral cover letter introduces a candidate and his or her credentials through a formal or informal introduction from a third party.

The most effective way to utilize the referral process is to ask the party referring you to make the formal introduction himself or herself. In other words, if a close former colleague knows Sam Johnson, head of purchasing at ABC company, I will ask my friend to call Mr. Johnson, endorse my candidacy for employment, and inform Mr. Johnson that I will be calling on him or sending him a resume. In the alternative I can contact Mr. Johnson first, but when he requests my resume, I will want to include a strong referral letter with my letter and resume.

JACK BRENDAN

P.O. Box 5326 • Murfreesboro, Tennessee 37133-0895 • (615) 555-3273

August 10, 1998

> *If you are requesting someone to write a letter on your behalf, you could show them this as an example. This is a very strong endorsement letter.*

William A. Bryce
Vice President - Information Systems
ABC Corporation
000 Beachside Way
Suite 3
Nassau, Bahamas WY1 988

Dear Bill,

I hope the reconstruction from the hurricane is progressing well. You and I will have to test out the links on my next trip into Nassau to review the accounts. Hopefully, the new course will be more forgiving to our level of golf game.

You had said when we last talked that the new network you are having installed would be done by December if you could find a project manager that was competent. I may be able to help in that respect. I'm enclosing the résumé of Scott Reed, an intelligent young man whom I feel you should meet and consider for your Director of Information Technology.

Scott has done some contract work for us here at Centraway on our network and workstations. I have been very impressed by his work. He has come up with some very good ideas for improving the operations of the department through some special training he's performed for our Help Desk personnel and IT staff. If projections turn out correctly, we should be saving around 450 hours a quarter on down time from the innovations in our procedures that Scott has introduced.

Scott has his CNE and the MSCE designation, plus he's fairly proficient in RPG so he can work on both sides of the system. He's had experience in managing LAN projects of the size and scale of the one you have slated for your facility, including the new fiber install/upgrade at our California location. He's done a great job for us and I think he might be just the thing to get your operation up and running down there.

Take a look at Scott's résumé and feel free to give me a call if I can provide any further information for you or details concerning the work that he's done for us here at Centraway. I'll hate to lose him as a consultant, but I know your operation there is in dire need of someone with Scott's excellent talent and skills.

Give my regards to Jenna. I look forward to our next meeting on the links!

Best regards,

Jack Brendan

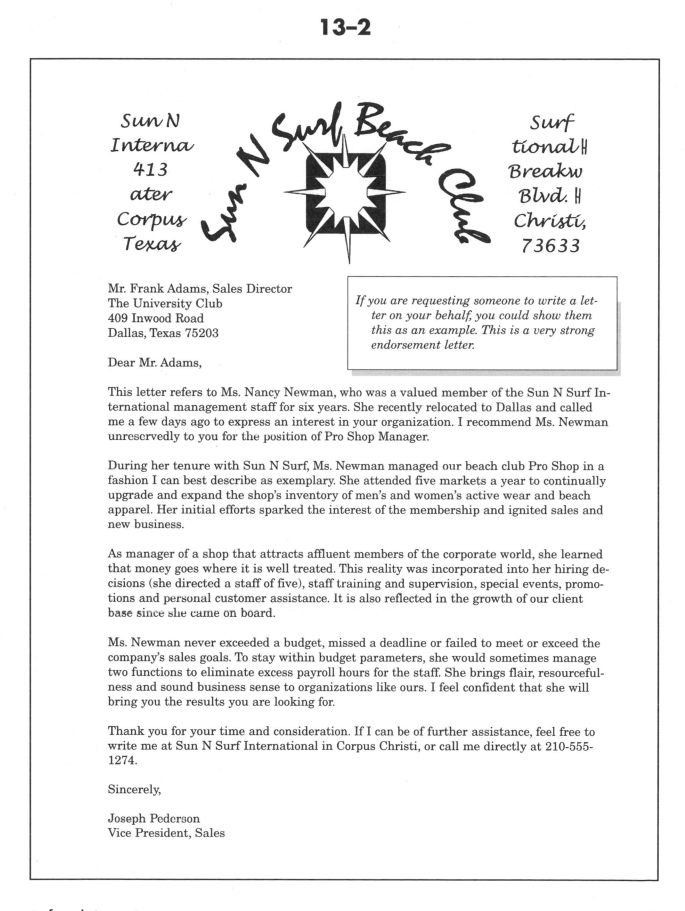

Sun N
Interna
413
ater
Corpus
Texas

Surf
tional H
Breakw
Blvd. H
Christi,
73633

Mr. Frank Adams, Sales Director
The University Club
409 Inwood Road
Dallas, Texas 75203

If you are requesting someone to write a letter on your behalf, you could show them this as an example. This is a very strong endorsement letter.

Dear Mr. Adams,

This letter refers to Ms. Nancy Newman, who was a valued member of the Sun N Surf International management staff for six years. She recently relocated to Dallas and called me a few days ago to express an interest in your organization. I recommend Ms. Newman unreservedly to you for the position of Pro Shop Manager.

During her tenure with Sun N Surf, Ms. Newman managed our beach club Pro Shop in a fashion I can best describe as exemplary. She attended five markets a year to continually upgrade and expand the shop's inventory of men's and women's active wear and beach apparel. Her initial efforts sparked the interest of the membership and ignited sales and new business.

As manager of a shop that attracts affluent members of the corporate world, she learned that money goes where it is well treated. This reality was incorporated into her hiring decisions (she directed a staff of five), staff training and supervision, special events, promotions and personal customer assistance. It is also reflected in the growth of our client base since she came on board.

Ms. Newman never exceeded a budget, missed a deadline or failed to meet or exceed the company's sales goals. To stay within budget parameters, she would sometimes manage two functions to eliminate excess payroll hours for the staff. She brings flair, resourcefulness and sound business sense to organizations like ours. I feel confident that she will bring you the results you are looking for.

Thank you for your time and consideration. If I can be of further assistance, feel free to write me at Sun N Surf International in Corpus Christi, or call me directly at 210-555-1274.

Sincerely,

Joseph Pederson
Vice President, Sales

14

Salary Histories

Often you will be asked to send a resume, cover letter, and salary history or requirements. Unless you have a good reason to do so or are specifically asked to do so, you should *not* volunteer salary information.

There are two ways to address salary information:

1. with a Salary History Addendum Page, or
2. by including the information in the cover letter.

When providing salary information you want to appear flexible, providing a rather generous window so as not to jeopardize your chances of making the first cut. One response might be, "My salary requirements are flexible and negotiable. Over the past seven years, in diverse environments, I have earned between $45,000 and $75,000."

Hester R. Swann

8950 Miami Trail
Cincinnati, Ohio 45242
(513) 555-3456
e-mail hrswann@aol.com

Salary History

1983 to 1985	Elder-Beerman Stores	*salary*	$18,000
	Retail Sales	*salary*	$22,000
	Department Manager	*performance bonus*	$3,000
1985 to 1986	Federated Department Stores Sales	*salary*	$18,000
	Director: Cosmetics	*performance bonus*	$17,000
1986 to 1990	Duramed Pharmaceuticals	*salary + commissions*	$42,000
	Sales Representative	*salary*	$60,000
	Southwest Sales Manager	*performance bonus*	$18,000
1990 to 1992	Forest Pharmaceuticals	*salary*	$75,000
	Regional Sales Manager	*performance bonus*	$37,000
1992-present	Phillips Medical Systems	*salary*	$90,000
	Divisional Sales Manager	*performance bonus*	$30,000
		salary	$155,000
	Director of Sales Development	*salary*	$165,000
	Vice President, Medical Sales	*performance bonus*	$32,000
		executive incentive compensation	$35,000

Easy to read and understand salary history matrix.

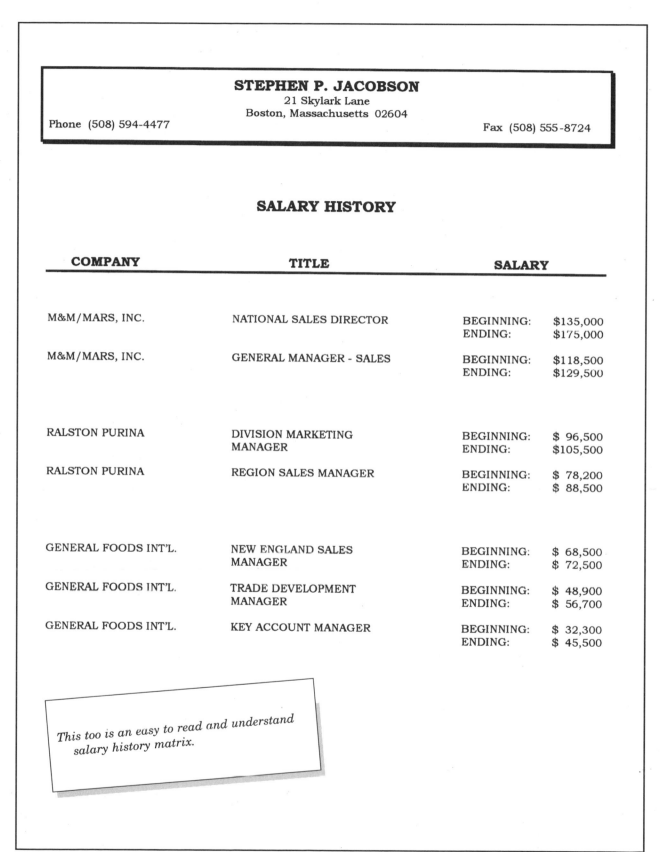

STEPHEN P. JACOBSON

21 Skylark Lane
Boston, Massachusetts 02604

Phone (508) 594-4477

Fax (508) 555-8724

SALARY HISTORY

COMPANY	TITLE	SALARY	
M&M/MARS, INC.	NATIONAL SALES DIRECTOR	BEGINNING:	$135,000
		ENDING:	$175,000
M&M/MARS, INC.	GENERAL MANAGER - SALES	BEGINNING:	$118,500
		ENDING:	$129,500
RALSTON PURINA	DIVISION MARKETING MANAGER	BEGINNING:	$ 96,500
		ENDING:	$105,500
RALSTON PURINA	REGION SALES MANAGER	BEGINNING:	$ 78,200
		ENDING:	$ 88,500
GENERAL FOODS INT'L.	NEW ENGLAND SALES MANAGER	BEGINNING:	$ 68,500
		ENDING:	$ 72,500
GENERAL FOODS INT'L.	TRADE DEVELOPMENT MANAGER	BEGINNING:	$ 48,900
		ENDING:	$ 56,700
GENERAL FOODS INT'L.	KEY ACCOUNT MANAGER	BEGINNING:	$ 32,300
		ENDING:	$ 45,500

This too is an easy to read and understand salary history matrix.

15
Follow-Up Letters

In many cases, the difference between success and failure in a job search is follow-up. Most people send out a resume and expect that someone will call in response to it. That is not a strategy that breeds accomplishment. Once a resume has been sent out, a phone call made, or an interview concluded, you should send a follow-up letter. (Sometimes, the follow-up letter will be in the form of a thank you letter; see Chapter 21.) The mission is to generate actions—interviews and meetings. Follow-up letters are tools to inspire such action when original tactics fall short of expectations.

Patrick M. O'Reilly

534 Madison Way, #21B
Farmingham, CT 06100

E-mail: PMOR@not.com
860- 555-7645

August 13, 1998

Mr. John Smyth, President
Smyth Insurance, Inc.
123 West Main Street
Hartford, CT 06111

Fax #: 860-555-6000

RE: **Customer Service** position

Dear Mr. Smyth:

As you suggested during our brief telephone conversation this morning, I am faxing to you my résumé in application for the **Customer Service** position advertised by your company. I have also mailed a hard copy of the résumé for your permanent file.

Thank you for your concise explanation of your needs. I know that my ten years of success in the insurance industry, analyzing and responding to customer queries, will help to raise customer satisfaction levels and enhance profitability for your own organization. My proven abilities are demonstrated by such achievements as:

♦ Hand-selected to represent my employer during a presentation to a new client company, because of my ability to answer benefits questions and explain claims procedures.
♦ Received monetary awards for superior quality and customer service.
♦ Salvaged a key account by improving speed and quality of service and follow-up.
♦ Received numerous letters of commendation written by satisfied customers.

I am confident that my strengths will help you to create a greater customer focus, which will in turn boost earnings and raise morale. Could we speak soon about my possible contributions to Smyth Insurance? Thank you for your time; I eagerly await the opportunity to meet with you in person.

Sincerely,

Patrick M. O'Reilly

Attachment

> *Notice how Patrick restates the needs of the company and draws the connection between those needs and his skills.*

15-2

6200 Thrasher Avenue, Chatfield MN 55923 ✆ **(507) 555-5555**

August 12, 1998

Ms. Shawna Dison
Manager
Rejuvenation, Inc.
902 N. Paget Drive
Milwaukee, Wisconsin 55555

> *Important use of immediately thanking the interviewer for her time and effort during the interview. Also, notice how Christopher restates his background that is relevant to the interviewer.*

Position of Interest: Assistant Manager of Healt

Dear Ms. Dison:

It was such a pleasure touring your health facility yesterday, and I truly appreciate the time spent from your busy schedule for such a lengthy interview. As mentioned, I am extremely interested in working for a firm of this caliber. The management style which you developed, in addition to the quality programs and equipment, are quite impressive.

My experience interning at the Mayo Clinic as a Health and Wellness Specialist has been invaluable, serving to reinforce my enthusiasm and interest in the field. I have been fortunate to work in positions that forced me to take a very proactive approach with clients. One of my key strengths is the ability to develop relationships which set clients at ease and encourage them to ask questions concerning their program, progress and goals.

Since 1992 I have been directly involved in the field, providing leadership in supervisory and management issues. You will note that my background is fairly broad-based, and I have experience setting up corporate wellness programs and training presentations. The NSCA certifications I hold in strength and conditioning, as well as in personal training, are of special pride. I feel these credentials would be of great benefit in assisting with staff coordination and oversight. Additionally, my experience managing operational expenses and scheduling at the Bedford Clinic provide a well-rounded complement of business skills.

Work ethic, dependability and integrity are high priorities with me, and I am very outgoing and professional in business and personal relationships. Self-motivated, enthusiastic, energetic and entrepreneurial, I manage with an eye toward profitability, growth and marketing issues.

I have already made arrangements with a Spanish tutor to refresh my language skills, and am excited about the opportunity to relocate to Texas. I look forward to touching base with you to discuss company hiring needs. If you need additional information, please let me know.

Sincerely,

Christopher Weston

ALICIA R. CEA

HOME: 972.555.5979
VOICE MAIL: 972.555.6339

10 A, COTTONWOOD COURT
IRVING, TX 76300

This letter is a follow-up from a networking meeting. Friendly and to the point, this letter keeps the door open for future contacts.

November 27, 1998

Ms. Allison Carter
Senior Vice President, International Operations
Republic Bank of Dallas
One Main Place, 59th Floor
Dallas, Texas 75200

Dear Ms. Carter:

Thank you. It was a pleasure to meet you and your wonderful staff yesterday. The tour of your impressive international service facility was an unexpected bonus!

As we discussed during our meeting, I am exploring possible assistant financial directorship opportunities in the Dallas/Fort Worth area. Having recently left my position with my family's Guatemalan corporation, I was concerned about my working knowledge of financial practices, policies and procedures in the United States. Thanks to your generous time and attention to my concerns, I have a greater understanding of this dynamic market.

On your good advice, I have decided to narrow my focus to international financial services, capitalizing on my multi-cultural education and experience. These benefits combined with my core competencies in corporate finance should make me a very competitive candidate.

I look forward to seeing you at the upcoming fund-raiser for KLRN. I am very grateful that our paths crossed at the last one. Thank you again for your personal interest in my career path and yes, I will be delighted to keep you informed of my progress.

Respectfully,

Alicia Cea

DESMOND P. JEFFERSON
11570 Peach Tree Lane
Marietta, GA 40115
(770) 555-6659

This is a follow-up letter to a phone meeting. Notice he takes the opportunity to document his feelings about human resource's sense of him being overqualified.

July 15, 1998

Yasmine Carlson
Director of Human Resources
KPMG
9845 Washington Avenue
Atlanta, GA 46551
FAX: (404) 555-8829

Dear Yasmine:

It was a pleasure to briefly speak with you earlier this week. As I mentioned in our conversation, I have known both Mark Lanson and Skip Peterson for a number of years and wanted to express my interest in the Marketing & Public Relations position, even though another partner is conducting the search.

I have the ideal combination of marketing and management experience necessary for this position. Throughout my career, I have designed and implemented a diversity of innovative sales strategies and programs to successfully identify new business opportunities and maintain long-term client relationships. Further, my knowledge of the Atlanta area marketplace is extensive. I know what works and how to get the most exposure from marketing and promotions. This expertise is the value I would bring to KPMG.

After reviewing my resume, perhaps you may think that I am "over-qualified" and my compensation exceeds the level of pay anticipated for this particular position. To put your concerns to rest, the opportunity to join an organization like KPMG is an opportunity I do not want to pass by. Although my compensation has averaged $115,000, my salary requirements are flexible considering future opportunities for growth within the organization.

I would welcome a personal interview to further discuss the search and am confident that the outcome would be beneficial to future KPMG business results. I appreciate you passing this information along.

Sincerely,

Desmond P. Jefferson

PAUL K. RATHER

432 First Street, Monroe, Michigan 48162   (734) 555-5432

May 23, 1997

This is a letter following up on a phone meeting. Paul takes the opportunity to restate career highlights.

Mike Thompson
Management Recruiters of Detroit
1125 W. Lincoln Avenue
Detroit, MI 48226-0876

Dear Mike:

I enjoyed speaking with you today about possible opportunities in the Oakland County area. The enclosed résumé briefly describes my 20 years of experience in Quality Assurance and Operations Management. I have an extensive automotive manufacturing background, including new program management and new vehicle launches. My experience includes both OEM's and suppliers.

Highlights of my experience include:

- A solid record of significant and measurable improvements in quality.
- Led a major steel processing firm to successful ISO 9000 Certification in November of 1996.
- Developed quality systems at plant locations that earned Ford, GM, and Chrysler Quality Awards.
- Strong TQM background, with experience developing Total Quality Management systems.
- Training and hands-on experience in SPC, Just-in-Time, and Continuous Improvement programs.
- International experience with a willingness to travel.

I would be interested in investigating any companies you may know of that would offer challenging opportunities for someone with my experience. Please contact me to discuss the particulars of any opening before presenting my name and qualifications to potential employers. I am looking forward to speaking with you further, and answering any questions you may have about my background.

Thank you for your help and consideration.

Sincerely,

Paul K. Rather

W. JOSPEH SYNOWSKI
1330 Bridgeport Way
Norfolk, Virginia 25503
(804) 555-0321

> *Brief letter that does a good job restating the needs of the company and how the candidate will make a good fit.*

May 22, 1998

Mr. David Babcock
Vice President of Sales
International Packaging, Inc.
124 North 15th Street
Madison, WI 53901

Dear David,

Thank you for taking the time to speak with me Saturday morning about the exciting sales opportunity with International Packaging.

After reviewing my notes from our conversation, it is evident that you require a dynamic person who will not only generate sales revenue, but also play an integral part in maintaining International's position as a "leading edge" supplier of world class packaging equipment. In my present role in Customized Canning's global sales organization, I do this every day.

It is also my feeling that understanding customers' needs and nurturing personal relationships, are key elements of success in "our" industry. These attributes have led to my success at Customized Canning, and would prove to be valuable assets in this position.

I look forward to the opportunity of meeting with you in Madison to further discuss how we could mutually benefit each other.

Sincerely,

W. Joseph Synowski

Robert S. Millhouse

7923 Sycamore Lane, Cincinnati, Ohio 45242
(513) 555-1234

August 10, 1998

> *Notice in the second and third paragraphs, Robert restates the needs of the company and verifies that he understands them and is a good fit.*

Edward F. Linnehan, Ph.D.
Technology Business Manager
The Haverhill Company
277 Main Street
Haverhill, MA 01851

Dear Dr. Linnehan:

My visit to Haverhill last week was exciting and most informative. Thank you for the time and information you shared and for your efforts in orchestrating interviews with so many people in the Technology area.

In particular, I greatly appreciated the opportunity to present a brief overview of a manufacturing challenge I faced, and your receptiveness to my candid views as an end user of Haverhill products. The technical environment, professional excellence, and commitment to continuous improvement so evident at Haverhill are very attractive to me, and I remain extremely excited about pursuing an opportunity with your company.

As a side note, Dr. Linnehan, I want to stress that I fully understand the need of a company to *sell* its products as well as to focus on technological innovation. You'll note that my track record shows strong accomplishments in both *technical* and *business* areas.

Our meeting at the end of the day revealed that my technical capabilities could fit into a number of areas at Haverhill. My conversation with Eleanor Andrews concerning laser technology and high-speed through-put leads me to believe that this is an area where you may have a need I can fill. However, I remain open to exploring a variety of opportunities to find the best match.

I look forward to hearing from you soon to continue our discussions.

Sincerely,

Robert S. Millhouse

enclosure

JENNIFER SMITH

P.O. Box 2225 • Murfreesboro, Tennessee 37133 • (615) 555-3273

July 29, 1998

> *Immediately thanks the interviewer for the meeting. Good recap of their needs and Jennifer's skills to meet them.*

Eva Parsley
Training Coordinator
Rutherford Corp.
0000 South Blvd.
Murfreesboro, TN 37128

Dear Ms. Parsley,

I want to thank you for the time you spent with me this morning discussing the position of Training Instructor for the Technology Program at the Dartmouth facility. I enjoyed our time together and found the information you shared concerning the position interesting.

There is a great deal of work to be done at Dartmouth in getting the new Technology program up and running. My experience would be a positive contribution to this effort as I have started new programs from scratch on three separate occasions. In my first year of teaching, I walked into a new facility and taught six separate courses without benefit of textbooks, materials, or curricula and a zero budget. That first year was spent developing a whole program and curricula, one of which was later adopted for company wide implementation. In England, I developed the Training Centre and Computer Lab from scratch and worked to integrate it into all programs throughout the company. Finally, in my interim position at Westwood, I essentially took over all responsibility of the technology training program and put it on the right track, establishing procedures, program outlines and scheduling classes.

My creativity, flexibility, and experience would be very helpful in not only developing the new program at Dartmouth, but also in supporting a new Director of Human Resources in dealing with program start-up and instruction management. There is a great deal involved in the first stages of program start-up, especially in the cross-platform, global training environment. My background would be a distinct advantage at getting the program off to a good start for everyone.

Again, thank you for meeting with me and affording an opportunity to discuss the position with you and Ms. Jennings. If I can answer any further questions, please feel free to contact me at the telephone number listed above. I look forward to speaking with you soon.

Best regards,

Jennifer Smith

16
Endorsement Letters and the Endorsement Portfolio

Reference letters are effective tools only when they are turned into endorsement letters. Reference letters simply attest to what you did in the past; endorsements promote you for future opportunities. *Webster's New World Dictionary* defines the word *reference* as, "the giving of the name of another person who can offer information or recommendation; referring or being referred." For the word *endorsement*, the *Dictionary* reads: "a statement, as in an advertisement, that one approves of a product or service; to give approval to; support; sanction." Endorsements are highly proactive letters selling, promoting, and endorsing a candidate to a prospective employer. They are a powerful sales tools that you can utilize today.

An endorsement is similar to the concept of celebrity sanctions of a product or service. For example, Candice Bergen promotes Sprint; Paul Reiser promotes AT&T; Shaquille O'Neil promotes Pepsi; Bill Cosby promotes Jell-O. Though you may not get the endorsement of Bill Gates, many professionals you know can give very effective endorsements.

THE ENDORSEMENT PORTFOLIO

An Endorsement Portfolio is a set of four to six letters from business or professional associates describing your skills, abilities, and qualifications, backed by quantifiable data and information, aggressively promoting you to a potential employer. Ideally, the makeup of the group of associates would be:

- Two superiors—promoting your value and your ability to perform, produce, and contribute to the bottom line and to organizational goals and objectives.
- One peer—endorsing your ability to work as a team member and leader.
- One subordinate—vouching for your training, coaching, and supervisory skills.
- Two clients or vendors—affirming your high-quality customer service and professional integrity.

Alter the above list to fit your individual needs, but try to key in on influential people who worked with you, know you well, and will support your job search efforts. This is *not* the place to include personal endorsements (unless you are a student or returning to the job market after an extended absence), but rather professional ones.

WHAT IF I AM CURRENTLY EMPLOYED?

If you are currently employed, obtaining an endorsement from anyone associated with your present employer may be a challenge or even impossible. If you worked for firms that have gone out of business or were purchased by another company you may find it difficult to obtain endorsements. In these and other cases you must depend heavily on former consultants or vendors for endorsement.

If you feel comfortable confiding in a superior at work but that person cannot endorse you as a representative of the company, you may ask him or her to provide a professional endorsement from a personal perspective rather than as an officer of the company. In addition, you may wish to pursue former superiors and peers for endorsement. Those you previously worked with are an excellent source for testimonials. Recent endorsements are best, but it is better to have former colleague endorsements than none at all. The main objective is to develop a portfolio of endorsements from people who can unequivocally promote your skills and abilities—your potential to contribute and add value to your targeted company.

Many people leave jobs and break all ties with their superiors and peers as well as with the organization itself. A word of caution is called for here: *Do not burn bridges!* For whatever reason you depart, you must leave yourself the ability to approach people for endorsements. You need to leave with your head held high. Do not depart on a sour note, but if you have already done so, mend fences! If you make a concerted and genuine effort, most former bosses, peers, and subordinates will support your career and job search goals by providing you with endorsement letters. Using a tactful approach, sincere communicating skills, and a lot of humility will help you obtain a powerful endorsement even under very difficult situations.

WHO WRITES THE ENDORSEMENT LETTERS?

Of course the letter is delivered under the writer's signature, but writers will likely want your help for two reasons. First, it takes a lot of time to sit down and create a letter like this. It will be most helpful if you can outline the top several points you want them to capture in the letter, such as a few key accomplishments and an intangible such as your management style. That way the writers don't have to spend a lot of time thinking of the subject matter. We wouldn't recommend writing the complimentary comments for them, but do give them the specific points to bring up. Then suggest they embellish; they'll know what to do, especially if they are for your success.

Second, give the writers some idea of how to spin the tone and subject. Give them some information about the position or company and help them position you in the most effective light. After they write the letters, ask them to send you copies, even if they send the originals directly to the employer or recruiter.

In the end it is recommended that you write the outline for the endorsement letter yourself. Superstars don't write the ads we see on television; advertising agencies and marketing departments do. You are your own marketing department unless you also hire marketing professionals.

TEN STEPS FOR DEVELOPING AN EFFECTIVE ENDORSEMENT PORTFOLIO

1. Identify four to six people to provide you with powerful references.
2. Contact each person and request that they promote your job search efforts.
3. Get the support and agreement that they will write your endorsement letters.
4. Outline the information to be covered for the endorsee.
5. Give the outlines to them and ask them to complete the letters by your needed date.
6. Try to review the letters before they are sent out. These letters are most effective, though, if the endorsees send them, not you.
7. Get copies of the endorsements for your records.
8. Photocopy the letters and distribute them with your resume or at an interview.
9. Bring or mail a thank-you note to your endorsee along with a manila folder. Inside the folder should be a copy of your resume and a copy of the endorsement letter. Request that the folder be kept handy for future reference calls.
10. After every interview, contact your references and inform them of an impending call so that they will be prepared to provide a verbal endorsement supporting the letter. Then make sure you stay in touch with your reference people.

You should also give serious thought to including your portfolio of endorsements when you distribute your resume. These endorsements are your personal "promotional team." Use them along with your personal sales efforts to obtain the desired opportunity. Thus, your endorsements become verifiers confirming the integrity of the information on your resume. Mention the inclusion of the endorsements as a postscript in your cover letter. For example, at the end of your cover letter include a statement like this:

PS: I have enclosed my endorsement portfolio with my resume to assure you that all information contained on my resume is truthful and accurate. Thank you.

Sample Cover Letter:

Claude S. Rebecca
185 Chair Street
Rumney, New Hampshire 06222
(603) 555-9191

April 4, 1999

Mr. Lawrence Bruce
American Office Supply
18 S. Hope Street
Plymouth, New Hampshire 06324

Dear Mr. Bruce:

Your former assistant, Lisa Ina, mentioned that you are looking for a warehouse manager. I believe you will find my credentials convincing. I have the experience, accomplishments, and character to maximize warehouse production and deliver peak-performance results. Please consider the following:

* Fourteen years warehouse management experience
* Managed small to large size warehouses with inventory ranging between $300K and $6 million
* Possess technical and computer skills to automate any size warehouse, improve efficiency and reduce inventory-level requirements while improving customer service
* Strong managerial and coaching skills — responsible for up to 83 employees
* Verifiable record for consistently coming in under budget

I read in a recent trade publication that AOS is expanding internationally. Though I have been an American citizen for the past thirteen years, I was born and raised in France, speak four languages fluently and am experienced in the shipping and receiving procedures of many European countries.

Though I am providing a detailed résumé, it cannot fully profile the manner in which I have been successful. This can only be accomplished during a face-to-face meeting where we can exchange information and examine whether there might be an employment opportunity of mutual interest. Please expect my call early next week to arrange such a meeting.

I look forward to meeting with you soon.

Sincerely,

Claude S. Rebecca

PS: I have enclosed my endorsement portfolio to assure you that all information contained on my resume is accurate and truthful.

Sample Resume:

Claude S. Rebecca
185 Chair Street
Rumney, New Hampshire 06222
(603) 555-9191

WAREHOUSE MANAGER
Specializing in the Office Supply & Equipment Industries

Overview:
Fourteen successful years experience in warehouse management. A solid work history supported by consistently achieving positions of increasing responsibility as a result of major contributions to the bottom line. Areas of expertise include:

- Automation, systems analysis, and computerization
- JIT & Limited Needs Inventory management models
- Strong professional association ties — member/past president of NWMA

Employment:
1992 - Present

Grand Mountain Office Distributors, Grand Mountain, New Hampshire
Warehouse Manager - Responsible for all warehouse operations for this regional office equipment supplier serving New England. Direct 18 employees through 3 line managers responsible for $388K of inventory.
* Automated warehouse operations, saving company $123K/year in carrying costs, with a complete payback on capital expenditures in 26 months.
* Reduced total payroll expenses 38% while reducing shipping errors.

1980 - 1992

United Office Supply, Burlington, Massachusetts
Warehouse Manager - Responsible for warehouse operations for national office supply company. Directed 83 employees at 4 locations through 4 location managers. Responsible for $11.3 million of on hand inventory servicing over 2,600 retail stores.
* Automated warehouse operations at 4 locations, researching, purchasing and assisting in the installation and set-up of equipment. Designed conveyor system that led to elimination of 6 non-productive positions.
* Helped re-design computer software to interface among all locations. Total inventory dropped $5 million (from $16.5 million to $11.5) as a result of inter-office integration and cooperation.
* Awarded Warehouse Manager Life Membership, by the National Warehouse Manager's Association (NWMA). Voted President 1985-88.

Education:
Bachelor of Science Degree: Business Technology Tufts University, Boston, Massachusetts

Languages:
Fluent: English, French, Italian and Spanish

Interests:
Exercise, tennis, white water rafting, reading and community cultural activities

Sample Endorsement Portfolio

ENDORSEMENT PORTFOLIO

1)   Mr. Irving G. Slavin, President
       United Office Supply
       123 Mileta Avenue
       Burlington, Massachusetts 01777
       (617) 555-0000

2)   Mr. Kenneth Newton, V. P. Operations
       United Office Supply
       123 Mileta Avenue
       Burlington, Massachusetts 01777
       (617) 555-0000

3)   Mr. Aaron Avery, Sales Manager
       United Office Supply
       123 Mileta Avenue
       Burlington, Massachusetts 01777
       (617) 555-0000

4)   Ms. Marissa Justyn, Warehouse Manager / Inventory Control
       United Office Supply
       123 Mileta Avenue
       Burlington, Massachusetts 01777
       (617) 555-0000

5)   Mr. Jeremey Pels, VP Sales
       Xerox Corporation
       2300 Xerox Place
       Waltham, Massachusetts 01116
       (617) 555-1122

6)   Ms. Francis Morris, President
       Portland Pen Co., Inc.
       99 Vannah Avenue
       Portland, Maine 01566
       (207) 555-9977

UOS

United Office Supply
123 Mileta Avenue
Burlington, Massachusetts 01777
(617) 555-0000

August 10, 1992

To Whom It May Concern:

Any company fortunate to have Claude Rebecca as Warehouse Manager has a true advantage in today's highly competitive economic climate. UOS has benefited from Mr. Rebecca's expertise in management, employee and customer relations for twelve years. His independent management style allowed UOS to grow 480% over a 12-year period, and Claude kept his warehouse operations one step ahead of the rest of the competition.

His ability to anticipate and quickly adjust to changing technologies has resulted in contributions to corporate profits in the millions of dollars during his tenure with UOS.

We all but begged him to relocate to our new headquarters, but he felt that relocation to Chicago would not be in the best interest of his family. He did, however, spend 2 months in the Windy City training his replacement.

A true professional, Claude Rebecca is an indispensable asset to any organization. His team leadership skills, together with his visionary expertise, are unparalleled. Please feel free to contact me personally should you require any further information.

Sincerely,

Irving. G. Slavin
President

IGS/adt

UOS

United Office Supply
123 Mileta Avenue
Burlington, Massachusetts 01777
(617) 555-0000

August 18, 1992

To Whom It May Concern:

I had the pleasure of working with Claude Rebecca over the past 6 years as his immediate superior. His analytical approach, technical expertise, and aptitude for anticipating and reacting to changing environments are unmatched. He has a special knack for taking preemptive measures in eliminating problems to allot more time planning as opposed to putting out fires.

When you hire Claude Rebecca you not only hire a competent management professional, you employ a man who is loved and respected by all. He gives credit to his team, tactfully corrects errors, and generates excitement, energy, and cooperation among team members. Like any true superstar he brings out a person's best so everyone can share in triumphs and challenges together.

In closing, those of us at UOS will miss him and always remember him. As President of NWMA, he made an impact on everyone he came in contact with nationwide. Allow him to impact your company. I only hope we will not have to compete against him in the future. Feel free to contact me at anytime regarding this endorsement (Home # 617-555-8822).

Sincerely,

Kenneth Newton
V. P. Operations

KN/fwt

UOS

United Office Supply
123 Mileta Avenue
Burlington, Massachusetts 01777
(617) 555-0000

August 29, 1992

To Whom It May Concern:

As Regional Sales Manager for UOS, responsible for annual revenues exceeding $50 million, the lifeline for our reputation and growth is customer service. The speed and accuracy of the delivery of products to our clients determines our success, and that depends upon efficient warehouse operations.

I have worked with Claude Rebecca for over 8 years. There is no greater team player when it comes to any type of management. He listens to all parties concerned, sees the big picture, and has the confidence and foresight to integrate everyone's ideas to come up with a comprehensive plan that works for the company. He will sacrifice his own beliefs when it comes to the good of the company. However, that does not often happen because he has such an exacting pulse on the industry specifically, economics and business in general.

I highly endorse Mr. Claude Rebecca. We lost him as our Warehouse Manager, but will never lose him as a friend.

Sincerely,

Aaron Avery
Sales Manager

AA/nop

UOS

United Office Supply
123 Mileta Avenue
Burlington, Massachusetts 01777
(617) 555-0000

August 29, 1992

To Whom It May Concern:

I was hired by Mr. Rebecca in 1983. Of the 12 interviews I went on, Mr. Rebecca was the most professional, trustworthy and honest hiring manager I confronted. He explained to me the pros and the cons of the job, and explicitly stated what he expected short and long term. He also clearly noted that he was there to train, develop, and coach us all to success.

Little did I know that ten years later I would be promoted and become the first female warehouse manager in the history of the company. Claude encouraged me to be the best I could be, taught me to think on my feet and strategically plan for the future. Today, I owe my success to Claude Rebecca. He is a firm, tough and demanding manager, yet fair, open and motivating.

I know of no better mentor for our department. He made work challenging, fun and exciting. As his replacement, I can only hope that my subordinates will feel half the respect and affection for me that we felt for him.

Sincerely,

Marissa Justyn
Warehouse Manager / Inventory Control

Xerox Corporation
2300 Xerox Place
Waltham, Massachusetts 01116
(617) 555-1122

April 29, 1994

To Whom It May Concern:

We have had the pleasure of associating with Claude Rebecca over the past 14 years with UOS and Grand Mountain Office Distributors. In my 30-plus years in the business, all with Xerox, I have never met a more professional, talented or personable warehouse manager.

He is a strong and formidable negotiator. He always has the best interest of his company at heart. He is fair and always looks for a win-win solution to any negotiation.

He is a loyal and dedicated professional who will enhance any company. His value, when measured against his peers, is truly head and shoulders above the rest. Xerox will be pleased to provide you with any additional information you need. Contact me at the above address, and I will quickly respond to your inquiries.

Sincerely,

Jeremey Pels
VP Sales

JP/pty

Portland Pen Co., Inc.
99 Vannah Avenue
Portland, Maine 01566
(207) 555-9977

May 12, 1994

To Whom It May Concern:

Portland Pen began operations in 1992 with zero sales. We had a new marketing concept that was different from anything existing on the market at that time. Most people resist change — not Claude Rebecca. He listened to our ideas, added some of his own, and, as a result, was instrumental in assisting Portland Pen to its current market position as a $6 million company poised to go international and positioned for explosive growth.

At a time when Claude Rebecca could have enjoyed the relationships he had with other firms, he saw he could maintain those relations while opening new markets. He got the President of his company to look at our program, negotiated a highly profitable arrangement for Grand Mountain Office Distributors and gave us a chance. Today, Grand Mountain Office Distributors sells over $125,000 of our product and has given us credibility in the market.

Claude saw the benefit to his customer and his company. He is a man of his word, a man of integrity and a bottom-line progressive management professional. He helped make Portland Pen what it is today and where it will go tomorrow. Anyone who hires him is truly fortunate to experience his professionalism.

Sincerely,

Francis Morris
President

FM/hdt

17
The Hiring Proposal

Equating the process of career design or job search management with self-marketing, you will find that key selling techniques are heavily emphasized. Procedures and techniques used by sales professionals are very similar to those you will want to use in selling yourself to a prospective employer. For example:

THE SALES PROCESS	THE JOB SEARCH
1. Identify sales prospects.	1. Identify the companies you want to work for.
2. Contact the prospects and provide information on the product or service.	2. Call for appointments, prospect your network, or begin a direct mail campaign.
3. Visit prospect and make presentation.	3. Employment meeting.
4. Attempt to close the sale on the spot.	4. Attempt to force a hiring decision at the end of the employment meeting.
5. Write and send a formal proposal.	5. Write and send a hiring proposal.
6. Follow up.	6. Follow up.

So the next step in your sales program is to prepare and submit a hiring proposal! What is a hiring proposal?

The hiring proposal is a formal, written proposal sent to the hiring authority following an employment meeting or at any other opportune time. This document is an actual proposal offering your services to the company or organization. In effect, you are telling the prospective employer that you have accepted them as your future employer!

The hiring proposal is highly effective when:

- You feel you might not be the strongest candidate for the job.
- The company may be unsure about making the commitment or have head-count constraints.
- You were not offered the opportunity following the interview.
- The hiring process has been delayed and you want to take charge.

It is also a strategy useful for creating a job that does not exist, but whose creation you believe would directly benefit the organization. Under the right conditions, it is also used to reinforce a successful interview.

MAKE THEM AN OFFER THEY CAN'T REFUSE

Submitting a proposal is acceptable practice for most other disciplines; why not for a job search? Although not often used in the employment arena, preparing a job proposal is an innovative and effective method of showing initiative. Creativity and initiative are viewed favorably by most employers. They show you are an enterprising individual, a take-charge, proactive person.

In today's competitive job market all job searchers must see themselves as self-employed. You should consider using every effective marketing tool in your arsenal to promote yourself to potential employers. A hiring proposal is similar to any other proposal. It is an effective promotional instrument that communicates specifically how you can contribute to an organization.

HAROLD RAY HANDLEY
Master Plumber

32 Green Street
Bristol, CT 14235
Mobile (203) 555-8820
Home (203) 555-8879

May 27, 1999

Mr. Glen A. Abrams
Abrams and Abrams Commercial Plumbing Contractors, Inc.
2499 Pinehurst Way
Bristol, CT 14228

> *Hiring proposals can be a strong closing step toward getting your desired job. The bulleted proposal section and paragraph immediately following puts the employer in a "no lose" situation.*

Dear Mr. Abrams:

It was a pleasure meeting with you earlier in the week, and I was very impressed with your company. It occurred to me, as I was driving home following our interview, that the position of Commercial Plumber is perfect for me. I believe I have the four main qualifications we spoke about:

1) Supervisory and organizational skills
2) Customer service and client retention management
3) Commercial plumbing experience (20+ years)
4) Business development skills

I am so sure that I am the person you are seeking, I would like to offer you a proposal:

> **I would join Abrams and Abrams Commercial Plumbing Contractors, Inc. for a probationary period of three months. In that period of time I will achieve the five main goals we spoke about:**
>
> 1) Develop/implement a <u>formal, written policy/procedure manual</u> for staff plumbers
> 2) Develop/implement <u>cost-effective training programs to improve technical skills</u>
> 3) Develop/implement a <u>measurable customer service program</u> to achieve 98% (or above) service rating
> 4) <u>Improve gross margins by 5%</u> through enhanced productivity and purchasing/inventory management without compromising quality of service
> 5) To significantly <u>reduce turnover and improve employee morale</u>

If, after the initial 90 days of probation, you feel my work exceeds your highest expectations, we would discuss a more permanent, long-term relationship based on performance. Furthermore, I believe I can help market and promote Abrams and Abrams Commercial Plumbing Contractors to the many contacts I have in this area. I am committed to being a contributing member of your team in business development as well.

I will contact you next Monday, after you have had the weekend to review this proposal. I believe it is a win-win situation for both your company and me, and I look forward to discussing this next week.

Sincerely,

Harold Ray Handley

MELISSA T. GOLDBERG
191 Piper Road
Philadelphia, PA 19108
(215) 555-0901 / Pipersweet@mainnet.net

> *Two-part letter proposal. Page two of the proposal is a more formal business-like proposal; the only missing link is the to-be-negotiated salary/fee structure. A proposal like this is a bold move and demonstrates confidence of the applicant.*

June 17, 1999

Ms. Kateland Y. Yarney, President
Kateland Sweets, Inc.
5300 5th Avenue, 11th FL
New York, NY 10024

Dear Kateland:

Once again, thank you for meeting with me at your corporate headquarters in New York. I must say I was impressed not only with your operation, but the high caliber personnel you have working for Kateland Sweets. It is certainly an environment I would love to contribute in.

Per your request, I have enclosed a "preliminary proposal" of how I can best serve your present and future needs. This is by no ways a complete, comprehensive document as I would require more detailed data and information to be more specific in the final proposal. However, I believe this proposal is a good starting place for future discussions.

I look forward to reviewing this proposal with you and to discuss next steps in implementing it at your earliest convenience. Once again, thank you for your interest.

Sincerely,

Melissa T. Goldberg

PROPOSAL FOR KATELAND SWEETS, INC.
Submitted by Melissa T. Goldberg

I.   Conduct in-depth competitive market assessment and analyze
   - Industry association reports
   - Consumer Reports findings
   - Competitive analysis, in-house

**Completed in first 30 days**

II.   Conduct three national focus groups to ascertain consumer demand
   - Southeast market
   - Northeast market
   - Western market

**Completed in first 45 days**

III.   Introduce three new "brand" products by year 2000
   - Modifying/enhancing existing brands
   - Replacing existing brands
   - Augmenting existing brands

**In production in first 6 months**

IV.   Work with Controller and Marketing in developing product budgets
   - Cost of capitalization
   - Cost of goods sold
   - Marketing and distribution projections
   - Return on investment / P&L / cash flow pro formas

**Completed in first 3 months**

V.   Present comprehensive business plan and proposal to Board Members
   - Feasibility and ROI
   - Long and short term strategies
   - Increase projections in total national and international market share

**Completed in first 4 months**

KATHLEEN F. GERBER

2341 Willow Street
Houston, TX 77002
(713) 555-5498

> *Very strong proposal that exudes enthusiasm in working for the target company. The "No Risk Proposal" in bold will have a lasting impression on the reader.*

July 23, 1999

Ms. Candice Grey, President
Sports Relief Therapy Corp.
4552 East Binder Avenue
Houston, TX 77023

Dear Ms. Grey:

Following our interview today, I walked away thinking, "This is the company I really want to work for." I was impressed with your facilities, operations and personnel. Most notably, however, was the philosophy of SRT - unwavering dedication to rehabilitation. I believe there is a close "fit" between your company's mission statement and my personal beliefs. Key words and phrases kept coming up over and over again that got me excited about joining your organization - "quality care," "going the extra mile," "teamwork" and "professionalism." I believe I can make a positive impact and would like to propose the following:

NO RISK PROPOSAL

1. I would join your company as a subcontractor for the first 60-90 days (assessment period).
2. You will have the opportunity to see my skills before any long-term commitment is made.
3. You will see my team-spirited personality and how I will effectively interface with your clients and staff.
4. I will be highly active in promoting and recruiting new business to SRT based on my strong contacts.
5. If, after the initial assessment period you are pleased with my work, we can discuss permanent employment.

In closing, I feel that my training and passions are working with sports-related injuries and that our approaches to business and rehabilitation are on an equal par. There is no risk to SRT - if, for some unforeseeable reason this is not a good fit, neither party has made a long-term commitment. But I am confident that this will not be the case. I believe that this opportunity affords us both the chance to achieve our respective goals and aspirations.

I will take the liberty of contacting you by week's end to explore what next steps are needed to consummate this mutually beneficial arrangement. Once again, thank you for your time earlier today. I look forward to speaking with you on Friday.

Sincerely,

Kathleen F. Gerber

ALESIA B. DARLING
Darling Interiors

120 South Lincoln Blvd. / Marietta, GA 30062
Phone: (404) 555-2600 / Fax: (404) 555-2601

April 26, 1999

Allan Gladstone, Vice President
Baldwin Corp.
1200 Baldwin Way
Marietta, GA 30060

> *Second paragraph gets right to the point of the company's problem / objective, and her solution. Companies like solution-oriented professionals, and a hiring proposal demonstrates aggressive and problem-solving attributes.*

Dear Mr. Baldwin:

I enjoyed our interview yesterday for the position of Project Manager. It occurred to me as I was driving home, that I would benefit your company in three major areas while saving Baldwin Corp. time, money, and unneeded personnel issues. Please allow me to submit the following working proposal.

The Problem: To oversee and coordinate interior design work for new headquarters
Solution: Subcontract the project out to Alesia B. Darling

Working Proposal For Discussion Purposes

I know you are seeking a full time project manager for this assignment and I can be that person. However, when the project is done, you will probably NOT need to keep this employee busy 40 hours a week as we had discussed. The solution would be to bring me on as a contractor - 40 hours a week for a period of two years. When the project is completed, I can be contracted to do more or the assignment is over and the position eliminated. In this way, you have no payroll taxes, benefits, etc. to deal with. If at anytime you are not satisfied with my work (highly unlikely given my track record), you can terminate our contract, and most of all, I will work as an independent contractor and would more likely gain the cooperation of your current employees as a consultant (for input and planning purposes) than as an employee perceived as new to the organization.

I would work exclusively for Baldwin Corp. (on a contractual basis), and would take on no new clients without written permission in advance from you. In the end, Baldwin would save time and money over the two-year period of time you have dedicated to this project - and I am sure the quality of work would be equal to or better than an in-house manager, due to the "objectivity factor" that we spoke of.

In conclusion, I believe this would represent a win-win situation for us both. I will call you next Thursday to arrange a meeting to discuss this. Once again, thank you for your attention to this matter.

Sincerely,

Alesia B. Darling

FRANK J. DEVINCI
45 Light Street
Las Vegas, NV 89013
(702) 555-7397

October 27, 1999

Mr. Derick Anderson, VP Operations
The Golden Slot Corp.
1200 Main Street
Las Vegas, NV 89022

Dear Mr. Anderson:

I left our interview today with such enthusiasm and energy, I thought I'd submit a proposal that would proactively outline how I see myself contributing to The Golden Slot Corp. I was impressed with your growth over the past 7 years, organizational commitment to excellence, and plans for the future. I would like to be part of this explosive growth and become a contributing member of your sales force. I feel very confident that I can expand your sales in areas outside of Las Vegas based on the strategic alliances, partnerships, and contacts I have established internationally. Assuming I am brought on prior to the new year, I would project the following "conservative" sales forecast for the year 2000 as follows:

SOURCE	ANTICIPATED REVENUES	QUARTER
Cruise ship revenues	$25,000	1st / 2nd
	$80,000	3rd / 4th
International gaming operations	$200,000	1st / 2nd
	$435,000	3rd / 4th
US Gaming operations	$50,000	1st / 2nd
	$125,000	3rd / 4th
Total New Revenue in first four quarters	**$915,000**	

I would also expect a 20-25 percent annual growth rate based on existing clientele, not including a 25 percent annual increase in new customers worldwide.

I would be seeking a base salary of $125,000 and a structured bonus program based on performance. There is no doubt that I can make a sudden and impressive contribution to revenues and growth for The Golden Slot Corp. Please expect my telephone call next Tuesday at noon. I will be faxing you additional documentation this week to support my numbers. In the meantime, if you need to contact me, my Skytel page number is (800) 555-2346 ext. 120.

Warm regards,

Frank J. DeVinci

Randall Nobel

1234 8th Street
Freemont, MI 40002
(505) 555-6722

March 13, 1998

> *Again, a strong move on the part of the job applicant to go for the close and make the hiring company a very low-risk offer. His statement of what their needs are will make a favorable impression on them. Understanding their needs is always critical.*

Mr. James Allen, President
JJ Allen & Company
123 32nd Place
Freemont, MI 44403

Dear Mr. Allen:

What an exciting day I had last Tuesday meeting with you and your employees, touring your plant, and discussing the position of Warehouse Systems Administrator for JJ Allen & Company. You are an energizing person, and an energizing environment is one in which I enjoy working.

You spoke in depth of the need to centralize the purchasing of JJ Allen & Company's five locations. Your personal goal to reduce inventory levels 20% while improving delivery schedules is admirable and I know I can be of assistance to you in attaining your objective.

I also received the impression that top management was seeking automated inventory tracking solutions. In order to improve customer service, the development and installation of an effective inventory tracking system is mandatory. This aspect is one I handled at two of the three companies for which I worked.

Additionally, I witnessed a work force of highly dedicated, hard-working individuals who epitomized the ultimate team players. I was impressed by their enthusiasm and would like to join your team.

I am so highly convinced that I can contribute immediately to JJ Allen & Company's goals, growth objectives, and current needs that I would like to offer my services to your firm on the following terms:

- I propose coming on board as an Inventory Control & Purchasing subcontractor for a 90-day period. Within the first 30 days I will convert JJ Allen's current inventory software into a cutting-edge program. This will enable you to see a 20% reduction in inventory by the end of the third month, along with improvement of customer order shipments from 87% to a minimum of 95% — guaranteed!

- I will work with all satellite location buyers to centralize the purchasing department. This will eliminate duplication of orders and reduce high shipping fees, enabling you to lessen payroll costs. Within this 90-day time frame, I will tighten up the purchasing process by reducing the price we pay, improving the terms of our agreements, and showing an overall increase in productivity. Eliminating *location buyers* will allow us to train and re-assign present buyers as inventory specialists; key personnel who will allow us to maintain low inventory levels while achieving near 100% service levels.

Randall Nobel
Proposal JJ Allen & Company
March 13, 1998
- Page 2 -

- I have had more than 7 years successful experience in designing and implementing automated warehouses utilizing a computerized conveyor system. This conveyor system picks and tracks the inventory via computerized robotics. Although I understand that JJ Allen & Company will not need such a system for at least a year, I will submit to you (within this same 90 day period) an initial design for this system, along with the costs and the cost-benefits of this type of system. A consultant's fee for this project alone would run $25,000 plus.

Mr. Allen, I have worked in this profession for over 15 years and have a solid reputation, including strong endorsements from industry professionals. The best endorsement, however, would be for me to demonstrate to you that I am the best person for the job.

At the end of this 90 day period, I will have demonstrated my value to JJ Allen. My proven commitment to your firm, along with my expertise and team-spirited management style will enable us to discuss a permanent employment opportunity at that time. I am certain you will be impressed.

I will call you by the end of the week to discuss this further. I enthusiastically look forward to our next meeting.

Sincerely,

Randall Nobel

18
Acceptance Letters

Upon being offered a new job opportunity, you may be asked to accept the job in writing. A job acceptance letter indicates that you are accepting the position and, in an enthusiastic way, reconfirms the terms of the offer.

MARY LOU MAKEPEACE
559 Union Boulevard
Colorado Springs, CO 80909
(719) 555-9050

July 13, 1998

> *An acceptance letter like this restates many points in a standard offer letter, as well as provides the hiring manager with the new employee's understanding of what is expected in that position (middle section of letter).*

Mr. Samuel Adams, Human Resource Manager
Board of Realtors® of the Pikes Peak Region
601 East Pikes Peak Avenue
Colorado Springs, CO 80903

Re: Acceptance of Position as MIS Manager

Dear Mr. Adams and the Board of Directors:

The purpose of this letter is to accept your offer of the position as Manager of Management Information Services. Pursuant to our previous discussions, my first day on the job will be Monday, August 10, 1998. In the intervening three weeks, I will be completing the training of my replacement at Holly Sugar Company.

The terms of employment as detailed in your letter dated July 10, 1998 are completely acceptable and I am enclosing an executed copy of that letter.

More importantly than start date and terms of employment - we are in complete agreement concerning the initial prioritization of my duties:

1 - resolve the problems of employee morale due the lack of leadership in the past two months and evaluate all present employees assigned to MIS with a specific goal to reduce assigned administrative staff by not less than 10%; and

2 - implement corrective actions to improve the timeliness and reliability of MIS reports available to Board Members together with special training sessions for Board Members who expressed their concern regarding understanding of these reports; and

3 - develop and implement enhancements to the BORIS system.

I anticipate objective 1 will be resolved within two weeks with a formal report presented to the Board before its August meeting on Friday, August 14, 1998.

I will see that a detailed report regarding the timeliness and reliability of reports will be available to the Board before its September meeting.

Finally, the third objective, developing and implementing enhancements to BORIS, will be an on-going function involving direct input from the Executive Director, the Board's Subcommittee on MIS and feedback from regular meetings of the membership, where, as promised, I will be available to answer questions and receive input from the membership as a whole. Success in attaining this objective can be measured directly by the reduction of complaints from members regarding BORIS and its complexity.

Sincerely,

Mary Lou Makepeace

Janine T. Edwards

98 Circle Boulevard
Madison City, FL 33888
(888) 555 -5432

March 25, 1999

> As written in paragraph 2, an acceptance letter can be a good way to document salary increase discussions held during the interview process.

Mr. Scott Adams
Vice President, Operations
Multiplex Manufacturing Company, Inc.
28 Technology Parkway
Sarasota, FL 33444

Dear Scott:

It is with sincere enthusiasm that I accept your verbal employment offer of March 24 to join the professional staff of Multiplex Manufacturing Company. To reiterate our agreement, I will begin my position as Senior Marketing Manager on Monday, April 12. As we negotiated, my compensation package will include a base salary of $52,000, a comprehensive health and insurance benefits plan, pension plan contributions, and participation in an annual bonus program.

In addition, I understand that we will meet to formally review performance and establish key objectives every six to nine months; at our first review session in October, we will discuss an increase to my base salary to more closely align it with the $60K I had articulated as my objective. This will be tied to achieving the specified performance outcomes we discussed in our meeting last week which you will be documenting in a memo to me.

Scott, based upon our meetings at the plant with the Director of Manufacturing, the R&D Engineer, and your sales staff, I am confident we can implement several highly effective programs targeted to significantly boost brand prominence for Multiplex in key market segments. As I commented in our last discussion, I've already begun to develop several preliminary concepts for moving plans forward. Let's schedule some time together on the 13th; I would like your input after I've had a chance to meet with my staff on Monday.

I am very excited about working with you and the rest of the team at Multiplex. Together, I am certain we can significantly grow the business and exceed the expectations of our directors and stockholders.

Best regards,

Janine T. Edwards

19

Letters Rejecting an Offer

Upon being offered a new job opportunity, you may decide **not** to accept it. When you make this determination you are either declining the job unconditionally or are open to further negotiations. A job offer rejection letter communicates that you are not interested in the position or are open to further discussion. In the latter case, you can outline specific terms more favorable to you.

Thomas B. Gallitto
Two Harvest Lane
Jordansville, IL 78222
(812) 555-2256

> *Gracious decline of job offer. Always more professional than just declining the position over the phone.*

April 10, 1999

Mr. David P. Johnson
Human Resources Manager
ATX Technologies
P.O. Box 28332
St. Louis, MO 68123

Dear Mr. Johnson:

Regretfully, I am writing to decline your firm's generous employment offer. Upon reflection and consideration of my personal and career objectives, I have determined that a relocation would not be in my best interest at this point.

I do sincerely appreciate the time you and Mr. Landry spent with me throughout the interview process to fully describe the engineering position and your operations.

Thank you for your consideration of my candidacy. I am confident you will identify an appropriate candidate. Please offer my best regards to the management team at ATX.

Sincerely yours,

Thomas B. Gallitto

MICHAEL AARON
115 North Union Boulevard
Colorado Springs, CO 80909
(719) 555-9050

June 12, 1998

Ms. Amelia Weatherspoon, President
Roth Medical Supply Company
135 North Cascade Avenue
Colorado Springs, CO 80903

> *Michael is sincerely grateful for the time expended during his interview process. He explains his reasons for declining the offer but tries to leave the door open for the future. This is a very good example of a letter declining an offer.*

Re: Healthcare Sales position

Dear Ms. Weatherspoon,

I want to thank you sincerely for the three interviews we have just completed. In each step in the interview process you have been graceful and forthcoming with answers to my questions and professionally demanding in the questions you have asked of me. Your offer yesterday of the position was received quite favorably.

As we discussed during each of our meetings, I have been in similar discussions with another organization. Kansas Healthcare Systems (KHS) has made a decision to enter the Colorado Springs market with a special product that has little interest to Roth Medical Supply.

After a great deal of thoughtful consideration, I have elected to accept a position as Sales Manager with KHS and must respectfully decline your most generous offer. I want to sincerely express my gratitude for the professional way you handled all of our dealings. At this point in my career I believe it is in my best interest to accept the position with KHS because it offers greater opportunity for financial rewards.

Because KHS will not be a competitor of Roth Medical Supply, I would like to keep in contact with you professionally since we both understand that there are also greater risks associated with accepting the position with KHS. I know that had I accepted your offer, we would have had an excellent professional relationship and I hope you are successful in finding a qualified candidate for the position as anyone should be honored to work for your organization.

Sincerely,

Michael Aaron

20
Letters of Resignation

When you have accepted a job offer while working for another employer, a letter of resignation to your current employer is in order. For the most part, these letters should be very brief in nature and show no animosity whatsoever. They should build on past successes shared between you and the company, as well as praise specific individuals.

There may be specific instances when you feel the need to be critical of some aspect of the past, but that is a professionally immature perspective. It is our belief that you should not put anything in writing that may be negative. Even though there are millions of people in the U.S., it can be an unbelievably small world at the city or industry level.

PAULA A. MUSTO, RN
1061 Campbell Street
Mansfield, Massachusetts 02048
(508) 555-3399

August 14, 1998

Ms. Patty Kirkwood, Nursing Director
Cardiac Intensive Care Division
Children's Hospital
3000 Longwood Avenue
Boston, Massachusetts 02115

> *Always praise the company as you exit. Offer to help in any way as you transition/leave, as well as making yourself available for future reference if they need your help.*

Dear Patty,

Probably one of the most difficult things in life is change, particularly a change that involves longtime friends and associates. This is one of those difficult times. Life has handed me new opportunities for career advancement as I join the staff at Memorial Hospital in Colorado Springs, Colorado and, as a result, I must submit my resignation.

It is customary in a letter of resignation to speak kindly and well of the employer and of one's co-workers. It is much more difficult however for me to communicate clearly the degree of absolute confidence I have in everyone at Children's Hospital. My tenure has been pleasant, involved the routine, the technical and the creative. I will especially miss the special learning opportunities you afforded me and the acknowledgments you made of my contributions.

I leave having learned a lot and, hopefully, contributed a lot. I will miss the interaction with you and other administrators.

Please accept my thanks for the guidance and training you provided me over the past eight years.

Sincerely,

Paula Musto

21

Thank-You Letters

More than a matter of class, it is a matter of common decency to thank someone who helps you. A thank-you letter, regardless of the magnitude of assistance, is always appreciated. Make it a habit to send one at every opportunity—following interviews, after phone calls from people who have been of help, networking meetings, referrals, and virtually any act of kindness by another person. Even a small item like a thank-you note can make a *big* difference in the outcome of your efforts.

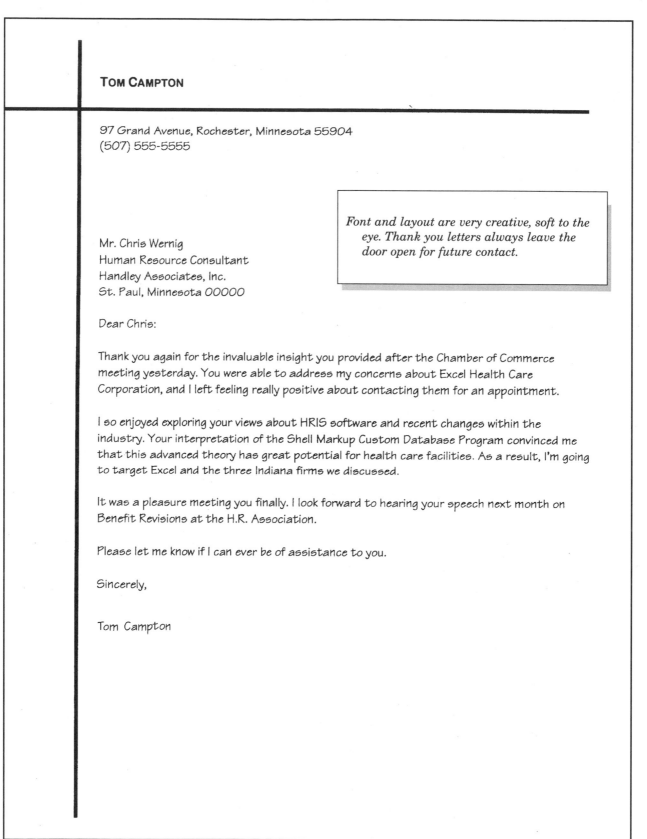

TOM CAMPTON

97 Grand Avenue, Rochester, Minnesota 55904
(507) 555-5555

Mr. Chris Wernig
Human Resource Consultant
Handley Associates, Inc.
St. Paul, Minnesota 00000

> *Font and layout are very creative, soft to the eye. Thank you letters always leave the door open for future contact.*

Dear Chris:

Thank you again for the invaluable insight you provided after the Chamber of Commerce meeting yesterday. You were able to address my concerns about Excel Health Care Corporation, and I left feeling really positive about contacting them for an appointment.

I so enjoyed exploring your views about HRIS software and recent changes within the industry. Your interpretation of the Shell Markup Custom Database Program convinced me that this advanced theory has great potential for health care facilities. As a result, I'm going to target Excel and the three Indiana firms we discussed.

It was a pleasure meeting you finally. I look forward to hearing your speech next month on Benefit Revisions at the H.R. Association.

Please let me know if I can ever be of assistance to you.

Sincerely,

Tom Campton

Elaine Cassinelli

7520 Mallard Lane, West Chester, Ohio 45140 • 513-555-7890 • ecass@aol.com

August 10, 1998

Rebecca Daniels
Director of Nursing
Inter-Health Services
105 Day Square
Hamilton, Ohio 45015

> *This letter shows gratitude toward the interviewer. She is focusing on building the relationship and leaving the door open for future contact.*

Dear Becky:

Thanks so much for suggesting that I contact David Knight about the in-service coordinator position at The Manor Nursing & Living Center. I met with David yesterday, and we had a very positive first discussion. I was impressed with The Manor's facilities and particularly its commitment to continuing education for both nursing and caretaking staff. As you know, it has always been one of my chief concerns to train, educate, and improve the skills of *all* the individuals who are caring for patients, and I was very pleased to hear this same commitment from several people at The Manor.

You will be pleased to know that David spoke very highly of Inter-Health and how easy it is to coordinate care for their residents who are also your clients.

Becky, I greatly appreciate your efforts on my behalf. I am very excited about this opportunity with The Manor, and I will certainly keep you informed of my progress through the interviewing process (I have a second interview scheduled next week with Pat McNeil, the Director). Whatever the outcome, I would be more than pleased to return the favor in any way I can.

Best regards,

Elaine Cassinelli

22

Internal Letters

Sometimes you must communicate within your organization for personnel reviews or if you are formally requesting a raise or promotion. All the letter-writing principles apply to these internal letters, with one exception:

> *Though you might exaggerate your accomplishments to outsiders in your resume and cover letters, be realistic in your assessment in internal letters, because whatever you write down will be very easily verified.*

We provide four examples of internal letters.

RAYMOND D. CHARLES

Residence:
(626) 555-9742

120 Western Avenue
Arcadia, CA 91006

e-mail: rcharles@flash.net

> *Notice how Raymond recaps his key accomplishments at his current employer. Never exaggerate your accomplishments on an internal resume or promotion/salary increase request.*

April 5, 1998

Mr. Wayne Graham
Vice President of Marketing
O'Sullivan Furniture Company
123 West Paradise Way
Los Angeles, CA 91045

Dear Wayne:

As you know, I have worked with you for two years as Electronic Marketing Manager of O'Sullivan's Business Furniture Division. As we discussed yesterday, I believe that my contribution to the company warrants an increase in salary. As my supervisor, you have been able to observe that contribution firsthand. But I felt it would be a good idea to take inventory of my achievements.

Here are the accomplishments of which I am most proud:

- Key player in helping O'Sullivan develop an aggressive Internet Marketing strategy to take full advantage of current technology.

- Pioneered strategies in electronic marketing. As you know, the Business Furniture Division was the first division to establish a Web presence.

- Conceptualized and created all aspects of our Business Furniture Web Page (including web site structure, design, coding, image editing, and copywriting) saving an estimated $57,000 in freelance designer fees.

- Developed a private web site to support sales force, with sales training materials, memos, newsletter, and logos. This site streamlined the marketing process and made the marketing department accessible to sales staff 24 hours a day. It also reduced sales paperwork by 40%. As you know, I have been asked to help Shipping & Receiving develop a similar system.

- Obtained additional training to keep my skills up-to-date, including Advanced JavaScript, HTML 4.0, and Microsoft Certification. These skills are currently in demand, and significantly improve my marketability in the workforce and my value to O'Sullivan.

Wayne, I look forward to continuing to work with you to move our company ahead with the unlimited marketing potential of Internet technology.

Sincerely,

Raymond D. Charles

ConnTran Telecommunication Services
Internal Memorandum

This letter is written as an internal memo, perfectly acceptable for internal communication. Excellent documentation of the Result for every skill or accomplishment.

To:	Steve Donovan
From:	Jessica Lewis
Date:	April 2, 1999
Subject:	Field Service Revenue Administration Manager's Position

Steve:

I am writing to formally express interest in being considered as a candidate for promotion to the position of Field Service Revenue Administration Manager. I have attached an up-to-date copy of my resume as well as a memo detailing salient project accomplishments over the past 18 months. I present the following highlights:

In my capacity as Lead Contract Administrator, a post I've held since 1997, I've demonstrated key managerial skills in these critical areas:

- Mentored three new Contract Administrators and facilitated formalized on-the-job training utilizing a comprehensive procedures manual which I conceived and authored. *RESULT* ... Increased proficiency and improved productivity via dedicated training program.

- Provided ongoing consultative support to acting RAM with numerous initiatives proposed to streamline administrative flows throughout the department via alignment of cost centers with dedicated CAs. *RESULT* .... Reduced revenue billing lagtime by more than five days and improved accountability to customers through focused CAs.

- Instrumental in successful implementation of conversion to automated batch processing through design of pilot program I created and launched while serving as interim RAM during January. *RESULT* ... Processing method has since been adopted company-wide by all revenue administration centers, substantially improving accuracy and timeliness of revenue flow.

In addition to these achievements, I believe you are aware that I recently completed ConnTran's intensive management development program, earning the training team's highest evaluation to date, a 4.98 on a 5.0 scale. This is complemented by graduate studies at RPI; I anticipate satisfying the degree requirements for a Master's in Business Administration next spring.

Steve, beyond my credentials and more than six years of progressive experience with ConnTran, I possess an unwavering commitment to our organization's success and a genuine desire to contribute to its dynamic leadership well into the next century. I look forward to speaking with you about your plans for this department and my ideas for effectively leading the revenue administration team. Thanks for your consideration.

Jessica Lewis

Power Points Marketing, Inc.
2995 Executive Drive, Brookfield, Oklahoma 55555
507/555-5555

> *This is a "proactive" letter reminding her supervisor of the past year's accomplishments as they enter into the merit raise period. Always make sure your self-evaluation is realistic.*

Date: July 8, 1998
To: Mr. James J. Robbins, Sr. Division Manager
From: Shawna Hinman, Manager of Eastern Region
Re: Performance Evaluation

In anticipation of our annual Performance Review Meeting, I have attached an outline of my accomplishments since July 30 of last year.

Exceptional sales people consistently outperform and outpace their competition. My fifteen years working for Power Points Marketing, Inc. have been marked by steady professional growth and achievement. I have learned from the ground up, working in almost every department before seeking a career position in Sales and Marketing. As the monthly performance figures show, each of the last five years I've exceeded company projections by at least 30%. I'm especially proud of the hard work that landed the Jones-Smythe account, a contributing factor to our 1997 growth and expansion.

While positive sales growth figures are essential to a company's overall goals, it is the stability and reduction of overhead that are essential to remaining competitive when the economy takes a sudden downturn or competition becomes especially brutal. Again, I'm pleased to have made important contributions in the last year to company budgetary tightening. The idea I introduced for restructuring the networked sales distribution system reduced that expense by 68%.

My achievements are the result of high productivity and creativity that surpassed company and personal goals. Consistent networking and rapport-building with customers and vendors added to this success. I have planned and executed sales and marketing programs, targeted high profit lines, accelerated revenue growth, developed and penetrated new markets. With self-motivation, high work ethic and enthusiasm, I have been very successful in motivating and inspiring the staff I coordinate and train. Because of strong training and leadership, I've had the pleasure of watching them grow in their own careers and successfully increase sales volumes.

I appreciate the periodic bonuses the company has awarded me in recognition of performance and excellence, and I am hoping that the enclosed report will be of assistance in calculating the 1999 salary levels. I feel that a raise is especially justified in light of the accomplishments and changes demonstrated in my performance in all areas of responsibility.

If you need additional information or figures prior to our meeting on the 27th, please let me know.

CARLTON MUNZER

Letter formally requesting promotion. Notice how the accomplishments chosen are verifiable within the organization and quantitative in nature. This is easy to do in the sales discipline.

Mr. Robert Fuller, Executive Vice President
Wagner and Poles
3429 First Avenue
Fort Lauderdale, Florida 33325

Dear Mr. Fuller:

As a seasoned sales manager with Wagner and Poles (4 years as Sales Manager, 7 years in total), I am armed with extensive expertise in developing new business, turning around sluggish sales and significantly impacting growth and profits. I believe I am well-qualified for the position of National Key Account Manager within our organization, and have enclosed a résumé outlining my highlights and contributions with regard to Wagner and Poles.

My strengths include developing my territory ($23 million and 7 sales reps) to peak levels of productivity through effective sales and management strategies. I possess a proven track record of realizing objectives in accordance with future goals. In addition to expanding a client base, my accomplishments include:

- **Achieving 125% of quota**
- **Penetrating previously closed markets and fostering communications with key accounts**
- **Recruiting, training and managing a dynamic sales force, each of whom has surpassed his/her personal quota**
- **Personally generating over $5.3 million in sales within the past year**
- **Attaining annual sales to the U.S. government of $1.5 million**
- **Securing accounts with both K-Mart and Avon through persistence and strong interpersonal skills**

Aggressive, tenacious and a true team player, I am enthusiastic about continuing my career with Wagner and Poles well into the 21st century and I look forward to discussing the position in greater detail.

Very truly yours,

CARLTON MUNZER

Enclosure

23

Consultative Sales Approach within the Job Search

In the last several chapters we've tried to show the parallels between the job search process and marketing a product. Marketing principles revolve around the four P's: product, place, promotion, and price. Your self-marketing principles should revolve around the same principles. Given that, it makes sense to draw the parallels even further.

Marketers attempt to create and position a product to meet the needs of their targeted sales segment. You too should position yourself in a manner that meets the needs of your targeted employers. Once marketers do the positioning, it is up to the sales force to complete the process. This is the place or distribution element of the marketing mix. Your sales element is in full force when you are in the interviewing stage, but even prior to that you need to set the stage for a strong sell.

In some industries sales are transactional, meaning that the sales department sells a commodity type of product, simply taking and filling orders. A company that provides long-distance service to businesses is a good example. It is selling a simple product that has many alternate vendors, and the product may have few differentiators other than price. The salesperson doesn't have to sell a concept or stress the relationship between the customer's needs and the product other than the ability to make calls for less cost.

However, what if the salesperson worked for IBM's consultative branch touting *Real Solutions,* selling an integrated solution that may include long distance along with managed network services, Internet access, data transport products, and WAN service? In order to make that sale, the salesperson would absolutely have to understand the needs of the customer.

Enter consultative sales. Consultative sales calls for you to really understand the needs of the customers (or your prospective employers) and convince them that you have a product to meet those needs. In order to rise above the pack in the job search process, you need to demonstrate to prospective employers that you clearly understand their needs and that you can meet those needs.

Here are areas to research about an organization. These are areas you should understand and research prior to beginning the cover letter or sending your resume, so you can address the items in your communications, just like salespeople and marketers do:

- existing products
- new products
- geographic presence
- climate of the industry
- competitive products and companies
- emerging trends both in the industry and within the organization
- profile of current staff
- profile of desired staff skill set
- key business or market drivers

There are many other possible areas, but the point is to learn about enough factors so you can better position yourself as someone who can help the company achieve its goals, rather than as someone who needs a job. The research should take place prior to writing the cover letter and resume, so you can customize those documents to meet the needs you uncovered.

You can learn about these areas in several ways. The Web is a great place to start to learn about an industry or organization. You can order the company's annual report or call various employees and ask them about the organization in the context of the items listed above.

When you have uncovered that information, you can use it in two ways. In your resume you should position, spin, or highlight your accomplishments that are consistent with the company's overall goals. Your cover letter is the vehicle for formally addressing what you have learned and how you can help the company meet its goals.

Please take a look at the following letters and look for the ways each letter opens with an understanding of where the company is and where it is going. Then look for the ways the writers connect the company needs with their skills. If you can master this concept you will be very successful not just in your job search but in your overall career.

TONI MASTERS
3232 West Collings Avenue, Windsor Heights, IA 50311 (508) 555-9526

March 2, 1999

> Letter opens with a statement of Toni's understanding of the employer's needs and what they are looking for. She then ties her skills to their needs. Good example of the "consultative approach."

Mrs. Shirley Snife, Chairperson
Windsor Heights Girls Softball League
99 Town Center Road, Dept. A-6
Windsor Heights, IA 50398

Dear Shirley:

It is no secret that Windsor Heights has developed a woman's softball program that is the talk of the state. I read in the local newspaper a week ago that there are more than 160 women participating in the league and that the emphasis on skills training is so intense that Windsor Heights has won the State All-star Championships in each of the past two years. It is a credit to you and your staff that you have met an important need in our community - namely providing our children with the resources and opportunity to compete in an area that they love to compete in.

I also read in that same article that you are looking for volunteers to coach these girls - that there are four or five openings for coaching and assist coaching positions. I have a fifteen-year old daughter who has played the last two years in the league. Having been an active parent, I think I have a good idea as to what you are looking for in a coach. I offer you the following:

1)   More than 11 years coaching experience as an Assistant Athletic Director at the high school level
2)   Able to grasp and teach the fundamentals of the game
3)   Ability to inspire players in a positive way, to give 100% and achieve peak-performance levels
4)   Teaching emphasis on sportsmanship
5)   To work with parents, league staff, and others involved in making this program a success

I know that there are limited head coaching positions available and I would very much entertain the opportunity to assist a head coach in hopes of demonstrating my abilities for a future coaching position.

I will be attending the Board Meeting scheduled for the 24th of this month and I hope to meet with you before the meeting to properly introduce myself to you. If you would like to speak/meet with me prior to the meeting, I will make myself available at your convenience.

I look forward to another great season and hope to become a participating member of your coaching staff.

Sincerely,

Toni Masters

CHARLENE W. PARKER
668 West Hannover Boulevard
Chicago, IL 60623
Phone: (718) 555-2486
E-mail: Fivestar10@Main.net

> *Notice how Charlene spends the first two paragraphs talking about them, not herself. In paragraph four, she draws out the connection between their needs and her accomplishments and skills.*

July 9, 1999

Mrs. Grace Billings, Customer Service Manager
United Parcel Service
1000 State Street
Chicago, IL 60602

Dear Mrs. Billings:

Congratulations on the recent contract between the pilot's union and management. The strike of 1997 was surely devastating, not only to UPS, but the nation as a whole who depend on and trust UPS. The agreement signed last week ensures that the good name of, and extraordinary service provided by, UPS will not be tarnished.

I read in the Business section of the Chicago Times, over a month ago, that UPS was expanding its call center operations in the Chicago area and that a "benchmarking" effort was going to be made to bring the center back in-house after many years of contracting the service. Now that the talk of strike has been put to bed, I am sure you will be focusing attention again on this project. I believe I can help !

I work as a Call Center Manager for Sears Roebuck and Company here in Chicago. They too once contracted out their call center / customer service operations and made the decision to bring it in-house six years ago. I was one of nine team leaders responsible for the strategic planning and implementation of the conversion from contracted to in-house call center operations for Sears. I was part of this team from the very beginning to now - where over a six year period we have improved our customer service rating from 93.7% to 99.2% while saving the company approximately $1.2 million. I have implemented a tactical plan to further enhance the rating to 99.7%, and now I am seeking new challenges.

Some of my career highlights include the following, which actually tie in closely with the emerging needs at UPS:

- Personnel management and team-building; directing a team to consistently exceed organizational expectations
- Systems and operational benchmarking; developing systems of operations that can be replicated in other operations
- A highly competitive but jovial manager who inspires success while demanding results
- Strong finance / budget management skills; bottom-line oriented

I am sure that you see connection between my five areas of strength above and the criteria by which UPS evaluates potential managers. I know your time is extremely valuable and so is mine. Therefore I would enjoy speaking with you for a few moments over the telephone to determine if an in-person meeting might be beneficial to us both. Please expect my call next Monday afternoon. If this is not a good time to chat for a few minutes, we can arrange another time that is mutually convenient.

Thank you for your time and consideration.

Sincerely,

Charlene W. Parker

Walt Johnson
2357 Indiana Lane • Indianapolis, Indiana 49877 • (317) 555-5687

First two paragraphs provide level-set of prospective employer's current situation. Notice how Walt waits until the middle of the letter to talk about himself.

September 8, 1998

Ms. Christy Garcia
Director Sales and Marketing, AT&T Data Services
3333 Westwood One
Indianapolis, IN 49557

Dear Ms. Garcia:

I have been researching AT&T and their play in the integrated services offerings for some time. I was intrigued to read about the upcoming INC announcement that is currently scheduled for this Fall. INC is reportedly going to converge data and voice transport products into a single, more cost effective single transport that can support virtually unlimited bandwidth demands.

In order to pull this off, you will surely need to have strong relationships in place with the CLECs or ILECs in given markets. In the short run that is the only way you can provide the local access "last mile."

I have a lot of experience working with Bell Atlantic/Nynex and Bell South in xDSL. xDSL will surely be your plan for last mile access when it is built out, and you will need skilled network data engineers to optimize and design that integration.

Please take a look at my resume, which reflects the broad experience I have developed in data transport and xDSL technology. I will call you next week for an appointment when we can review this further.

Sincerely,

Walt Johnson

Peter Parish

2357 Golf Drive Lane
Coppell, TX 75220
(817) 555-5974

June 9, 1999

Mr. Grant D. Powers, CEO
Golden Bear International
Golden Bear Plaza
11712 U.S. Highway 1
North Palm Beach, FL 33412

> *Strong opening with mention of common acquaintance. Establishes that he understands their current situation and needs before talking about himself.*

Dear Mr. Powers:

Your Controller, Mr. Gerald Haverhill, told me over golf a few weeks ago that you are looking for an MIS director. He told me some very interesting things about GB and I was impressed, not only with the growth and profitability but in the similarities between GB and Diversified Centers, my current employer. GB has added 23 new training centers in the U.S., as well as oversee the design of all Jack Nicklaus courses. With that much widespread activity, MIS needs must surely be exploding.

With that much national activity, you must need each site to be networked with your home office for both voice and data transport, as well as establish an WAN to improve real time connectivity. As well, the design aspect of the business must eat up a lot of bandwidth in data transport, so it would surely help if you could share information more quickly and efficiently, while maintaining your privacy "firewall."

My current operation is quite similar. I have built a very efficient network for our many regional locations to communicate. Diversified Centers builds and manages strip mall shopping centers for Tom Thumb grocery stores. Our network enables each regional office to stay in touch via email and shared drives through our WAN, as well as utilize the Sprint ION network for real time communications of high bandwidth development plans, similar to your use of golf course designs.

It appears that my accomplishments with Diversified Centers is in line with your MIS needs at GB. I will give you a call next week to set up a meeting to talk further.

Looking forward to meeting you,

Peter Parish

PS - Gerald told me you are quite close with Mr. Nicklaus. Please congratulate him on his fine Masters showing !

CAROLYN KELLENBURGER

5534 College Parkway, Cape Coral, FL 33410 (941) 555-9753

Strong opening with mention of common acquaintance. Uses real, verifiable and easy to understand examples of accomplishments that directly relate to the employer needs.

March 15, 1997

Ms. Kimberly Houston
Paramount Pictures
4800 Hollywood Boulevard
Santa Monica, CA 90211

Dear Ms. Houston:

Jim Talley at Touchstone recently informed me that you are overseeing costumes and makeup for the new film, "The Nutty Professor." Jim shared with me some of the effects that you are planning to use transform the lead character between the thin professor and the very overweight professor. In order to pull this off, you will undoubtedly need artists skilled in this field.

Experience with plastics, makeup, special wraps and the various maskings take a great deal of skill to apply in a way that is transparent to the viewer. I know; I was the lead artist for several movies and clips, including Michael Jackson's "Thriller" video, Halloween H20 and in several "Tales from the Crypt" episodes.

My experience is very consistent with what you will need for your upcoming film. Please review my attached resume for the specifics of my film credits. You will see that I would be a good fit for helping you with all of the makeup and related preparations for the demanding transformation scenes. I will call you next Tuesday and set up a time to stop by the studio to meet you.

Sincerely,

Carolyn Kellenburger

Christine Pantoya ·

9981 Southern Boulevard • West Palm Beach, Florida 33409 • (561) 555-5719

March 29, 1999

First two paragraphs provide level-set of prospective employer's current situation. Notice how Christine waits until the middle of the letter to talk about herself.

Ms. Theresa Mascagni
Vice President Technical Operations
4800 Oakland Park Boulevard
Fort Lauderdale, FL 33341

Dear Ms. Mascagni:

After completing much research on the wireless communications industry over the last few months, it has become apparent that NextWave holds a unique position in the market. NextWave has secured multiple C-Block licenses across the country, and when built out will have a national presence comparable to AT&T and Sprint.

In order to meet your aggressive growth goals of launching this market by next Fall, you will certainly need a strong RF team that has experience in the CDMA platform. Specifically, you will need a team that has experience optimizing the Lucent and Nortel base stations.

As a consultant, I led RF teams from network design to launch with both PrimeCo and Sprint PCS in the Chicago and Dallas MTAs, both of which were on a Lucent platform. I can provide excellent references from both. I think NextWave is a cutting edge operation, one in which ingenuity, creativity and drive can make a material impression. I want to be a part of your team.

My experience is in perfect line with your needs right now and what you will need after launch. I will give you a call next week to set up some time for us to talk further.

Sincerely,

Christine Pantoya

MISTI DEORNELLAS

45227 Michigan Avenue, Chicago, IL 24197 (312) 555-3125

March 9, 1999

Notice how Misti spends the first two paragraphs talking about them, not herself. In paragraph four, she draws out the connection between their needs and her accomplishments and skills.

Ms. Maria Lane, Executive Vice President
Hyde and Smithson Public Relations, Inc.
1800 Scenic Way
Mountain View, VT 19877

Dear Ms. Lane:

Over the last few months I've noticed your firm moving into consulting with several healthcare firms. After speaking with Tom Aimee, I am aware that you are bidding on the upcoming opening of two new Columbia hospitals. You will no doubt need significant healthcare industry expertise to drive this account. Healthcare can really get complicated when trying to balance aggressive marketing and sales techniques along with a more public entity image.

The two new locations in Portsmouth and Springfield will be delicate openings given the amount of bad press Columbia has received in the last year or two. Columbia has been in trouble with both the IRS and FBI for tampering with federal aid and overbilling to Medicare. They will undoubtedly need good advice on how to position their openings to get off on the right foot.

I have been working in marketing and public relations for 9 years, most recently with Humana in Florida. We successfully opened 11 new hospitals over the last six years, and even experienced a storm when we opened the one in Orlando. That one opened in the midst of a major city-wide controversy regarding the for-profit nature of Humana versus the for-the good-of-the-people persona hospitals have maintained. Under my direction Humana successfully overcame that encounter and now that hospital is one of the most successful in the region.

My skills are very much in line with the needs of both your firm and your clients:
- 15 years in public relations
- 15 years in the healthcare industry
- Expertise in new launches and crisis management
- Key contacts within the industry

Please expect my telephone call in the next week so that we might be able to set a time to meet and discuss employment possibilities that would serve our mutual interests.

Sincerely,

Misti DeOrnellas

23-8

JAY B. LAWRENCE
21 Lighthouse Way, Nubble Light, ME 02779   (707) 555-9375 Jblawrence21@aol.com

May 30, 1999

> *Notice how Jay opens by capitalizing on the mutual acquaintance, and follows by spending the first two paragraphs reviewing their current situation. Then he states his skills in a way that ties directly to the needs of the company. Good letter.*

Mr. Paul Graves, Executive Vice President
Horrace Small Manufacturing
120 Opreyland Commercial Park
Nashville, TN 46732

Dear Paul:

Bob Harris let the cat out of the bag! I think it is the best long-term interests of our industry that Horrace Small Manufacturing enter the retail segment of the law enforcement uniform industry and compete with the other manufacturers who have begun to travel this road. There is no doubt, you will assume a leadership role in the retail operations as you have in the manufacturing arena. And I believe I can contribute to this success.

I have enjoyed working with you and your company over the past nine years as a vendor and retail client. We have certainly shared some great success stories together. When I first began Professional Image Uniform Company in 1990, few people gave me a chance to succeed, but Hoarse Small (Bob Harris in particular), the giant of the uniform industry, saw my potential and accepted me as a retail customer. Today, nine years later, Professional Image Uniform Company is one of the largest uniform companies in the nation. We even bought out Simons Uniforms, a company that tried to thwart our success. I am proud of what we accomplished and feel no regrets about selling the company to FSS, Inc., because I am now seeking new and more exciting challenges.

Might that challenge be to spearhead your national retail operations?

Bob mentioned that you are presently looking for a retail manager to direct operations at your flagship location. I would be interested in meeting with you to discuss this exciting opportunity. I have one more week to finish up things with FSS and then I am available to meet with in Nashville. I will call you tomorrow to discuss this fax.

There are six areas of accomplishment that truly do connect closely with the needs of Horrace:

1) An industry-recognized track record for successful retail start-up management - conception to implementation
2) Multiple retail operations management
3) Creative sales, marketing, and promotions tactics to accelerate growth
4) Inventory management expertise to ensure 5-star customer service with minimal inventory levels
5) Competitive positioning - understanding competitive influences and developing tactical strategies to be #1
6) Organizational/personnel leadership; hiring "attitudes" and inspiring peak performance

Paul, thanks for taking the time to review this note. I'd really love to get together for a few minutes soon to talk a little more. There is no doubt in my mind that we'd make a great team in pursuit of your retail growth objectives.

Sincerely yours,

Jay B. Lawrence

HELEN R. HENDERSON
21 Village Street
San Francisco, CA 99465
(302) 555-6102

February 22, 1999

> *Always leverage a common acquaintance as Helen has done. Notice how she states their needs in both their business and employees. She proposes the time frame for the first meeting, rather than wait for the employer to make the first move.*

Ms. Alice Greene
Center Plaza Hallmark
201 Broadway, Center Plaza
San Francisco, CA 99427

Dear Ms. Greene:

Bonnie Taylor provided me with your name and suggested I contact you regarding summer employment this season. Apparently, Bonnie has worked for you for the past three summers but will be in Europe this year and thought I might work in her place.

I understand you are looking for people who have experience in retail environments, are customer service oriented, are loyal and dependable, have working knowledge of point-of-sales computer technologies, and are drug free. Retail environments like this can be so difficult to find good people. The retail stores I have worked with at school have really struggled to get good, bright and courteous people to staff.

I am in my third year at UCLA majoring in Business Administration. As well, I have five years retail experience (The Body Shop, Wolfe Camera, and The Gap) and am very familiar with POS computer systems.

I will be off for the summer as of May 29th. However, I will be home for Spring Break (April 7-15) and would like to stop by and introduce myself to you. We can both be sure that Bonnie would not have introduced us to each other if she didn't feel I could fill her shoes in a way that measures up to your high standards.

I will call you next week to see if we can arrange an interview during my Spring Break. Thanks in advance for your consideration.

Sincerely,

Helen R. Henderson

CYNTHIA E. GOODMAN

2121 East 75th Street
Fort Lauderdale, FL 33304
(954) 555-5945

> *Restates previous meeting to establish instant rapport. She states her qualifications in tandem with the employer's needs. She assumes the responsibility of following up for their meeting.*

March 21, 1999

Mr. Howard Finelaw, President
Valet Services of South Florida
9205 Dixie Highway, Suite 200-B
Pompano Beach, FL 33360

Dear Mr. Finelaw:

Our paths have met on at least two occasions and I was truly impressed each time. Please allow me to explain. I attended the Executive Women's Association gala event three weeks ago at the Cypress Creek Marriott where more than 400 people attended. When I drove my car to the valet, I was awestruck by the professionalism of the attendants, the uniforms, and the courtesies extended, not only to me, but to everyone. I mean to say that the valet service was so exceptional, it was the talk of the evening!!

When I asked to speak to the hotel manager to rave about the valet service he told me that it had nothing to do with the Marriott. I found out that your company is responsible for this level of service. Last Saturday night I went to the Kravis center to see Phantom of the Opera. Needless to say, half of South Florida was there - and so were you!! Again, I could not believe the level of service provided - simply exceptional.

So our paths have met on two occasions over the past 4-5 five weeks - and I'd like to propose a 3rd. I am a highly successful sales professional and I will only represent companies with top-rated products and services. I would like to propose a meeting to discuss how I can best help your company grow and prosper even beyond the success you have had to this point.

After completing some research online, I discovered your website. I noticed that your company has plans to expand into Broward County as well as Martin. I know I can use my plethora of corporate contacts to help you build your company. And if you decide you want to go regional, state, or national - I have the experience and verifiable track record to assist in this area as well.

And here's the best part - I enjoy being compensated for results, and I guarantee results. I do not require a high base salary compensation plan, but actually prefer an attractive commission program. I am a six-figure earner and am only compensated when I bring in the business. My past sales experience has been focused on hospitality-oriented business, so I have key contacts with companies that can use professional valet services. In fact, I have spent the last three evenings studying the valet business and have familiarized myself with the competition, past and future trends, and growth/profit potential. Based on my preliminary findings, you are in a niche market with almost unlimited potential.

I have enclosed a detailed resume of my qualifications and will contact you early next week to discuss possible scenarios for future employment with your company.

Thanks for taking the time to read this letter. I do hope we can meet in the next week or so.

Sincerely,

Cynthia E. Goodman

Encl: resume

24

Keywords

Keywords are descriptive words, usually nouns, that are associated with specific disciplines or industries. Keywords are important because they are considered standardized for specific industries. For example, if you were an accountant, keywords might be cost accounting, budget analysis, auditing, tax, etc. Keywords can be critical in the worlds of software management and job searching. Employers and recruiters may take your resume and cover letter (especially if you sent them electronically) and scan them for whatever keywords they are looking for. For example, a finance director for Microsoft might scan resumes and cover letters for the words listed above, and if those words aren't on your materials you could miss the first cut.

That said, it is our belief that scanning and electronic searching of resumes and cover letters is more hype than a part of most corporations' practices. OCR software still isn't that accurate, and based on our research with many hiring managers and recruiters, scanning isn't done very often in practice. Keywords probably play a larger role in the real world in the scenario described below.

Keywords can be very important outside the computer search arena. In many cases, the initial scan of resumes is completed by either a human resources person or an assistant to the hiring manager. Even the most competent people performing this function can only do a good job of it if they are not intimately involved with the position or are not hiring for themselves. That is why it is important to keep a certain "boilerplate" aspect in your resume.

A client of ours named David Robinson comes to mind. He worked for PrimeCo Personal Communications and was curious about an advertisement he saw for a position with Ericcson. We updated his resume in a new style, like that on page 209. The key to that resume style was the use of the left column for a listing of accounts; that really becomes the core of the resume if you work in an account-driven environment like sales. The hiring manager called David for an interview and told him: "We've had so many resumes that I told my assistant not to bring me anymore unless they look like a perfect fit. The way you listed your accounts on the first page of the resume was a great way to show us who your contacts are." So the initial screening was conducted by his assistant, who was only scanning resumes for key items (words, industry-specific terms, product names, etc.), and his resume effectively illustrated his sales accounts.

Don't make readers work to learn what you're all about. Even in a 4 percent unemployment environment, the competition for good jobs is too stiff.

As you can see, keywords are not limited to just descriptive nouns, but can be any term that in a terse manner tells the reader about you and your skills. Below is a broad list of keywords that are discipline-oriented. It is by no means a complete listing; there are many, many more. At the very least you will get a sense of what we're talking about by reviewing this list. Not included in this list but just as important are the names of other companies or products, as illustrated in the above example.

Accounts Payable	Accounts Receivable
Administration	Administrative Assistant
Administrative Support	Advertising
Architecture	Artificial Intelligence
Asset Management	Asynchronous Transfer Mode (ATM)
Auditing	Backbone
Bookkeeping	Brand Image
Budgeting	Business Development
Call Center	Case Management
Cash Management	Catering
Cellular	Chemical Engineering
Chemical Scientist	Chief Executive Officer
Chief Financial Officer	Chief Information Officer
Chief Technology Officer	Clinical Studies/Services
Commercial Banking	Commercial Credit
Competitive Intelligence	Contract Administrator
Contracts	Copyediting
Copywriting	Corporate Communications
Corporate Development	Corporate Image
Cost Accounting	Cost Center
Cost Reduction	Credit
Credit and Collections	Customer Loyalty Programs
Customer Retention	Customer Service
Data Communications	Design Engineer
Director of Finance	Director of Information Services
Director of Information Technology	Director of Marketing
Director of Public Affairs	Distribution Channel

E-Commerce

E-Mail

Employee Relations

Equal Employment Opportunity (EEO)

Executive Presentations

Financial Planning

Focus Groups

Food Cost Control

Frame Relay

Full Time Equivalent (FTE)

Government Affairs

Group Manager

Home Healthcare

Human Resources

Investment Analysis

Investor Relations

LAN

Leasing

Litigation

Managed Care

Market Development

Marketing Management

Media Relations

Merchandising

MIS

National Accounts

Nuclear Engineer

Occupational Health

Order Processing

Plant Manager

Press

Product Development

Product Marketing

Profit/Loss Statement

Public Relations

Purchasing

Quality Training

Recruiting

Regulatory Manager

Research Specialist

Return On Equity (ROE)

Risk Management

Sales Management

Electrical Engineering

Emerging Technologies

Environmental Engineer

Event Management

Executive Secretary

Financial Restructuring

Food and Beverage Management

Foreign Exchange

Fraud

Fundraising

Graphic Design

Healthcare Administrator

Hospitality Management

Insurance

Investment Banking

Labor Relations

Law (with all derivatives)

Legal Affairs

Loan Processing

Manufacturing Engineer

Marketing Communications

Media Buys

Meeting Planner

Mergers/Acquisitions

Multi-Hospital Network

Not-for-Profit

Nursing

Office Management

Personal Communication Services (PCS)

President

Primary Care

Product Manager

Product Support

Project Manager

Public Speaking

Quality Control

Radio Frequency Engineering

Reengineering

Research

Return On Assets (ROA)

Return On Investment (ROI)

Sales Administration

SEC

Service Mark

Staffing

Systems Engineering

Team Leader

Telemarketing

Trade Shows

Training

Turnaround Specialist

Vice President

Voice

WAN

Software Engineer

Strategic Planning

Systems Leader

Telecommunications

Telesales

Trademark

Transportation

Underwriting

Video

Volunteer

Web Design

25

A Word about Resumes

Generally, writing cover letters and writing resumes go hand in hand. We take this opportunity to give you a brief overview of resume tips here, but for a comprehensive review you should pick up one of our resume books, *101 Best Resumes* or *More 101 Best Resumes*. There are many resume books on the market, but what most distinguishes ours are the resumes themselves. They are very focused on leading with value-added accomplishments rather than old-school objectives or summaries.

That brings us to our most important tip about resumes: They should promote your *accomplishments* like a marketing brochure would promote its product. Your resume should incorporate the Five P's, as we discuss them in our other books:

- **Packaging:** The resume has to look good to keep the reader going. Packaging is still very important, though lessened, in the electronic environment.

- **Positioning:** The resume has to be laid out in an easy-to-read format, which is physical positioning. Other positioning deals with how you *position yourself* in the resume. Are you positioned as an industry leader, a knowledgeable resource, dedicated, on the fast track? You need to understand your skills and goals in order to most efficiently position yourself.

- **Punch or Power Information:** This is the "meat and potatoes" that the hiring manager wants to see.

- **Personality:** Get creative and try to break out of the box of all those other boring and uninspiring cover letters and resumes.

- **Professionalism:** Use as much personality as you can, but you must remain professional in the process. The image you project on paper determines how you will be perceived in the job.

Do you notice the parallels between these P's and those in marketing? Make no mistake, conducting a proper job search has everything to do with successful marketing.

Starting on page 196, we offer ten of our favorite resumes from our two resume books. They clearly illustrate the Five P's, along with some creative layout formats.

25 "WHAT DO I DO NOW THAT I HAVE MY RESUME?" TIPS

1. Develop a team of people who will be your board of directors, advisors, and mentors. The quality of the people you surround yourself with will determine the quality of your results.

2. Plan a marketing strategy. Determine how many hours a week you will work, how you'll divide your time, and how you'll measure your progress. Job searching is a business in itself, and a marketing strategy is your business plan.

3. Identify 25 (50 would be better) companies or organizations that you would like to work for.

4. Contact the companies or do some research to identify hiring authorities.

5. Define your network (see Networking Tips). Make a list of everyone you know including relatives, friends, acquaintances, family doctors, attorneys, and CPAs, the cleaning person, and the mail carrier. Virtually everyone is a possible networking contact.

6. Prioritize your list of contacts into three categories: 1) strong, approachable contacts; 2) good contacts or those who must be approached more formally; and 3) those whom you'd like to contact but can't without an introduction by another party.

7. Set up a filing system or database to organize and manage your contacts.

8. Develop a script or letter for the purpose of contacting the key people in your network, asking for advice, information, and assistance. Then start contacting them.

9. Attempt to find a person or persons in your network who can make an introduction into one of the 25 or 50 companies you've noted in tip 3.

10. Spend 65 to 70 percent of your time, energy, and resources networking, because 65 to 70 percent of all jobs are secured by this method.

11. Consider contacting executive recruiters or employment agencies to assist in your job search.

12. If you are a recent college graduate, seek assistance from the campus career center.

13. Scout the classified advertisements every Sunday. Respond to ads that interest you and look at other ads as well. A company may be advertising for a position that does not fit your background but may say in the ad they are "expanding in the area," etc. You have just identified a growing company.

14. Seek out advertisements and job opportunities in specific trade journals and magazines.

15. Attend as many social and professional functions as you can. The more people you meet, the better your chances of securing a position quickly.

16. Send out resumes with customized cover letters to targeted companies or organizations. Address the cover letter to a specific person. Then follow up.

17. Target small to medium-sized companies. Most of the opportunities are coming from these organizations, not large corporations.

18. Consider contacting temporary agencies. Almost 40 percent of all temporary personnel are offered permanent positions. Today, a greater percentage of middle and upper management, as well as professionals, are working in temporary positions.

19. Use on-line services. America Online, Prodigy, and CompuServe have career services, employment databases, bulletin boards, and on-line discussion and support groups, as well as access to the Internet. This is the wave of the future.

20. If you are working on your job search from home, be sure the room you are working from is inspiring, organized, and private. This is your space and it must motivate you!

21. If your job search plan is not working, meet with members of your support team and change the plan. You must remain flexible and adaptable to change.

22. Read and observe. Read magazines and newspapers and listen to CNBC, CNN, and so on. Notice which companies or organizations are on the move and contact them.

23. Set small, attainable weekly job search goals. Keep a weekly progress report on all your activities. Try to do a little more each week than the week before.

24. Stay active. Exercise and practice good nutrition. A job search requires energy. You must remain in superior physical and mental condition.

25. Volunteer. Help those less fortunate than you. What goes around comes around.

Harry Ankenbaur

16 Oak Tree Road
Collinsville, Illinois 62234
(618) 555-4448

Senior Banking Executive

Retail Lending / Collections / Property/Facility Management

Senior Operating Executive in the banking industry with proven leadership skills and expertise in refining credit quality, returns on investment and capital, cross-marketing, asset growth, and analysis of risk-adjusted returns on mortgage lending. Successfully orchestrated the successful centralization of lending, collections, underwriting, and loan processing procedures to maximize asset performance. Early background includes regional operations and training management for a St. Louis-based investment company, supervising offices in 12 Midwestern states.

Career Highlights

BANK OF ALTON, Alton, IL, 1993-Present

Senior Vice President/Lending Officer

Recruited to bolster the lending operation for this community bank established in 1956, now serving 25,000 customers with $170 million in total deposits.

- Centralized the Collection and Secondary Mortgage Departments. Sold real estate loans in the Secondary Market totaling more than $20 million from 1993 to 1995. Collection of recovery accounts exceeded charge-offs for the last 3 years.
- Increased loan outstanding from $63 million to $106 million.
- Decreased classified loans from $10 million to $3 million.
- Implemented an Indirect Lending Department now serving more than 3,000 loan customers.

CENTRAL BANK, Fairview Heights, IL, 1980-1993

[formerly known as Southern Illinois Bank (SIB), purchased by Central Bank System, Inc. (CBSI) in 1985 and sold to Firstbank of Illinois Company in 1991]

Senior Vice President/Retail Lender

Provided leadership for Indirect Lending, Direct Lending, Collections, Property Management and Facility Management departments. Supervised 42 employees. Following the 1991 merger of two United Illinois Bank branches, formulated centralization of all collections into a single department servicing more than 16,000 retail loan accounts with a total net outstanding of $289 million.

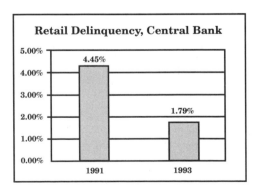

25-1

CENTRAL BANK, Fairview Heights, IL, 1980-1993
(cont.)

Supervised Property Management, including 11 facilities complete with a warehouse operation and a courier system operating between all locations.

Appointed Security Officer for the eleven locations in 1992. Established a written Security Manual conforming to the new Security Act and presented training sessions at all locations.
- Reduced retail delinquency from 4.45% in 1991 to 1.79% in 1993.
- Assumed additional responsibility of servicing all commercial collections deemed a Workout Status. Accepted the responsibility of managing the Bank's Other Retail Estate Owned (ORE). Reduced ORE from $1.1 million to $700,000.
- Centralized the Indirect Lending area into a single location servicing 46 auto dealers in the Metro-East area. With two underwriters and a clerical staff of four, processed more than 1,000 applications each month. Purchased $11 million in auto loan paper in the first three months of 1993 for a net gain in outstanding of $3 million.
- With the centralization of the collection department, reduced the amount of chargeoffs from 1.67% in 1991 to 0.85% in 1992.
- Implemented the Empirica Scoring System and a Quality Evaluation Guide to ensure quality asset growth and significantly reduce chargeoffs. Decreased 1993 1Q bankruptcy filings 50% compared to 1992 1Q.
- Centralized all Direct Lending into a single department processing approximately 200 direct loan applications per month. Provided a centralized approval process for Central Bank's 11 locations.

Vice President (1986)
Assistant Vice President (1980)
Successfully organized and set up a Secondary Mortgage Department for Central Bank in 1989. Originally started this effort with myself as the sole underwriter for FNMA. Formulated a staff that grew the department to $12 million in FNMA loans and serviced the direct real estate loans totaling $60 million. FNMA delinquency was zero when I left Central Bank.

Civic Involvement

- Illinois Center for Autism, 1989-Present; Chairman of the Board 1992-1993
- Salvation Army in Belleville, Board of Directors, 1989-Present
- Fairview Heights Rotary, Past President and holder of the Paul Harris Foundation Award; Proclaimed Rotarian of the Year in 1990
- Served as the District Treasurer for the Student Exchange Program in 1989
- Appointed to the Economic Development Commission in 1989
- Quest - Served on the Board of this Belleville Diocese Retreat Program
- Served on the Teens Encounter Christ (TEC) retreats for high school students for 10 years
- St. Henry's Parish - Finance Committee since 1991

Education

- Graduate of Illinois Bankers School of Southern Illinois University
- Applied Banking Diploma, American Institute of Banking
- Participated in Lending Management with Schesunoff
- Conference Leadership Training Course, American Investment Company

References Available Upon Request

Coleen S. Kubeck

21 East 39 Street, Apt. #3
New York, NY 10016

voice ■ 212-555-5555
fax ■ 212-111-1111
e-mail ■ ColeK@aol.com

Senior-level General Management in Modular Manufacturing Processes

Executive Profile

■ Over ten years of senior-level experience in astute business analysis and profitable management of 20 million dollar custom manufacturer. Forecast sales trends, enhance revenue streams, turn around troubled operations, and achieve profitability in down-trending markets. Administer all manufacturing, marketing, and environmental control functions. Supervise staff of up to 25 direct and indirect reports.

■ A hands-on manager and critical thinker who can learn quickly, develop expertise, and produce immediate contributions in systems, analysis, business operations, and motivational team-management. Possess a valuable blending of leadership, creative, and analytical abilities that combine efficiency with imagination to produce bottom-line results.

Proven Areas of Knowledge

■ business planning / development	■ operations management	■ operational troubleshooting
■ revenues and margins	■ multiple project management	■ task analysis
■ modular manufacturing architecture	■ facilities management	■ capital / consumable purchasing
■ trend and competitive analysis	■ crisis management	■ high-expectation client relations
■ joint venture formation	■ environmental management	■ training and development

Executive Highlights

■ Produced exceptional company growth, increased gross margin, enhanced productivity, and set new quality standards through the proactive design of innovative programs, sales techniques, and manufacturing methodologies as well as the imaginative use of unique suppliers.

■ Doubled company's accounts and quadrupled sales by design and implementation of profitable value-added services. Division generated unit sales per employee that were 1.5 times that of the industry's largest independent service bureau. Produced division turnaround time of 10 to 12 weeks vs. industry average of 13 to 18 weeks.

■ Created an innovative in-house service bureau, the only one of its kind in the industry. Produced new revenue streams representing 12.5% of sales through pro-active marketing of new service bureau as a quasi-independent operation that gained new cross-industry, non-printing accounts.

■ Avoided purchase of multi-million dollar computer graphics system through inventive utilization of offset and reprographic service bureaus, reducing expenses even further by scheduling projects in bureaus' down-times.

■ Designed and directed company's strategy to prevent major losses from 40% erosion of customer base during late 80's recession. Spearheaded production of proprietary nationally distributed wallcovering collections, advertising, and collateral materials. Developed manufacturing relationships with large furniture producers and cosmetics firms. Marketed color separation and film services to competitors.

■ Prevented massive disruption in service by assuming immediate control of all manufacturing operations in crisis response to key administrators' mismanagement and subsequent departure.

Coleen S. Kubeck

Employment History

Distinction Printing, Ltd., Long Island City, NY — 1980 to present

Company manufactures custom wallcoverings, decorative laminates, large-scale graphics and point-of-purchase specialties, with a peak sales volume of $20 million and a number two ranking in this specialized industry of twenty contract wallcovering printers in the United States.

Vice President and General Manager — 1995 to present

Assumed control of all manufacturing operations following departure of two key managers. Situation required immediate action to position company to recover from mismanagement. Downsized staff, slashed overhead, cross-trained personnel, instituted strict housekeeping controls to curtail waste, and reduced inventory — all with no reduction in quality.

Increased margins by 60% on four existing customer collections, signed with two new national distributors, and developed high margin accounts. Increased business without increasing expenses through the use of vendors' sales people as a de-facto sales force to market company's services to non-competing screen-print industries.

Manage facility operation and safety / environmental coordination. Supervise all facility functions including hiring of contractors for maintenance and renovations. Administer vital hazardous materials program for entire corporation, including training, compliance, documentation, and reporting. Directed all repairs, contractors, and insurance affairs after partial roof collapse and flooding in 1996.

Sales and Operations Manager — 1987 to 1995

Held full P&L responsibility. Increased division sales by 30% between 1987 and 1990 and steered company through the recession of the late 80's / early 90's when fully 40% of the industry's customer base was lost through consolidation and bankruptcy. Researched and developed new markets, created new opportunities as outsourced producer for competitors' small runs, and positioned company as fast-turnaround specialist.

Pre-Press Manager — 1980 to 1987

Planned production, scheduled, procured consumables, capital equipment, and outsourced-services. Created value added services that directly contributed to doubling of company's account base and quadrupling of sales from 1980 to 1987. Ran division turnaround times typically 30% less than industry standard, with no decline in quality.

Education and Development

Masters of Business Administration, New York University, New York, NY, 1990

Bachelor of Arts in Business Administration, State University of New York at Stony Brook, 1979

Technology

Use PC word processing, data base and spreadsheet software (MS Office), the Internet and E-mail.

Easily learn specific industry systems and software. Familiar with Mac, especially graphic arts software.

Everett Morris
50 Trouble Drive
Fairview Heights, Illinois 62208-2332
(618) 555-8228

Graphic/Visual Arts Specialist

Seventeen years' experience managing and coordinating visual arts projects from concept to completion. Accustomed to working on multiple projects with short notice, little or no instruction, and total creative judgment for quality and details of finished product.

- Well-rounded business management skills, with proven ability to match customer needs with a wide variety of graphics, visual arts tools, and approaches.

- Effective at communicating ideas and capturing the interest of the intended audience.

Professional Experience

Visual Information Specialist   1989-Present

(self-employment under contract to the Defense Information Technology Contracting Office, a full-service telecommunications and information systems procurement office with 400+ employees supporting the entire DoD and 56 non-DoD organizations)

Managed all operations of a $100,000 business supporting telecommunications, information systems, administrative, financial, and management staff. Responsibilities included record keeping, accounting, budgeting, and inventory control.

- Prioritized customer requirements and assigned workload to meet changing contract specifications and customer deadlines.
- Provided detailed instructions to employees for new, difficult or unusual requirements. Ensured quality of completed products prior to delivery to customers.
- Served as a concept consultant to assist and advise customers on colors, content, and size of finished products.

Additional Experience (1979-1989): Held the same title of **Visual Information Specialist** as a contract employee without the business management responsibilities.

Education

Graphique Commercial Art School, 1978-1979
St. Louis, Missouri

General Coursework, Belleville Area College, 1976-1978
Belleville, Illinois

Everett Morris - Page 2

Creative and Technical Skills

Paste-Up

Designed and produced paste-ups and artwork for illustrative slides, viewgraphs, and charts used in formal presentations, static displays, cover brochures and posters used for briefings to senior military and civilian personnel, static displays at trade shows, and various reports.

Engraving/Signmaking

Designed and produced plastic and metal engraved signs and plates used for organizational awards, plaques, and other recognitions. Designed and produced vinyl/plastic signs for badges, nameplates, name tags, cubical identification, and hallway directories.

Audiovisual Displays

Maintained audiovisual equipment library including the distribution, setup and operation of video and still cameras, audio recorders, overhead transparency, 16mm and 35mm projectors for presentations and training sessions.

Computer/Graphic Design

Designed and produced slides, charts, and graphs for weekly staff meetings and formal presentations using various software packages such as Harvard Graphics, Freelance Graphics, and PowerPoint. Manipulated color and size of clip art with software packages such as Arts and Letters. Produced forms, flyers and publications using PageMaker and Corel Draw software.

Presentation Planning

Provided expert consulting service to assist customers in presentation planning for the various types of media used to market, publicize and document the organization's goal and services. Used Harvard Graphics and Microsoft PowerPoint extensively.

Photography/Video

Provided video/audio and still photographic coverage of formal ceremonies, training, presentations, and satellite downlink training broadcasts. Produced working copies for approval by the customer and master and distribution copies of all materials. Provided photographic darkroom development of film, photo enhancement of prints in both black and white and color.

JENNIFER R. DOUGLAS

1808 Duncan Way
Nashville, TN 37211

e-mail: hairstylistgalore @ aol.com
Phone: (615) 555-9201

AWARD-WINNING HAIR STYLIST
Licensed Cosmetologist

A dynamic, highly creative, and seasoned hair stylist professional offering 16 years of award-winning hair design in major markets including Los Angeles and Boston. Recognized for successfully blending outstanding hair styling techniques with strong business development, customer service, and client retention management skills.

HIGHLIGHTS OF EXPERIENCE

- Recipient of the REGAL Award for outstanding styling and hair design, 1992 - 1998
- First place in regional styling competition sponsored by Paul Mitchel products, 1997 and 1998
- Instructor/consultant for more than 80 individual hair stylists and 14 hair salon owners between 1987 and 1998
- A verifiable track record for solid networking and marketing skills in building a strong client base in multiple markets
- Consistently generate client bookings exceeding $2,100 weekly in both the Los Angeles and Boston markets
- Provide back up management and sales/marketing/promotional support to beauty salon owners
- An excellent trainer and mentor to new, up-and-coming hair styling professionals

PROFESSIONAL EXPERIENCE

JEAN PIERRE RAFFAEL'S HAIR CLINIQUE, Beverly Hills, CA   1992 - 1998
Senior Hair Stylist / Public Relation & Marketing
PAMPER YOURSELF, INC., Beacon Hill/Boston, MA   1987 - 1992
Senior Hair Stylist/ Make-Up Artist
DIAMOND BEAUTY SALON, Arlington, MA   1985 & 1986
Internship: Hair Stylist/ Make-Up Artist

EDUCATION & TRAINING

MASSACHUSETTS BARBER AND HAIR STYLING COLLEGE, Brookline, MA
Master Hair Styling License, 1986

Courses and Additional Training :
- Advanced Hair Styling Techniques, Los Angles Hair Styling School, Los Angeles, CA, 1989
- Certificate of Completion: Cosmetology, Northeast Technical School, Boston, MA, 1990
- Hair Replacement Week-long Seminar, Danielle Wilcox School for Hair Replacement, Burlington, VT, 1995
- Hair Replacement Refresher and Update Seminar, Danielle Wilcox School for Hair Replacement, Burlington, VT, 1997
- Advanced Hair Coloring Techniques, Redken Symposium, Las Vegas, NV, 1998

LICENSES

Master Hair Styling and Barber License, California (#103729-AL)
Licensed Cosmetologist, Massachusetts and California (inactive)
Licensed Cosmetologist, Tennessee (active)

Professional References and Portfolio Furnished Upon Request

SUE SENTELL, FMP

19 East Main Street
Waterville, ME 56339
(222) 555-1212

SUMMARY

- ■ **Accomplished Hotel Executive** with 20 years' experience in food service field; hold distinguished FMP credential.
- ■ Consistent track record of successfully turning around faltering operations and creating profitability and excellence; utilize keen assessment and problem-solving abilities, dynamic training techniques, and key motivational strategies that build accountability and enhance staff performance.
- ■ Flexible, adaptable style and hands-on approach; a skilled manager who thrives in an atmosphere demanding excellence, autonomy, and strong team-building skills.
- ■ Possess highly polished communication and interpersonal skills.

PROFESSIONAL EXPERIENCE

1990–Present

Marriott Hotel and Conference Center • Bangor, ME
General Manager
Complete management responsibility for hotel operations with P&L responsibility for Food and Beverage department. Oversee facility including full-service restaurant, room service, lounge, pool bar, grand ballroom, three junior ballrooms, and 14 conference rooms. Overall facility comprises 30,000 sq. ft. of meeting space, banquet facilities servicing up to 1,600 guests, and 214 guest rooms.

Select Accomplishments ...
- • Achieved "Hotel Group Food and Beverage Hotel of the Year Award" (1997) on the basis of exemplary performance throughout all facets of operation (guest services, food and beverage, and overall profitability).
- • Named "Marriott Hotels Worldwide President's Award" winner (1995) for significantly exceeding guest satisfaction standards and overall performance measurements for hotel.
- • Overseeing facility-wide renovation ($4 million) scheduled for completion 1999.
- • Implemented comprehensive cross-training program complemented by development of in-depth job descriptions and accountability for all personnel.

Corporate Food & Beverage Consultant (1992–96)
Concurrent with management responsibility for the Marriott, served as Food and Beverage Consultant for hotels managed and operated throughout the United States by the Marriott's holding company, ABS Hotel Associates.
- • Implemented comprehensive cost control systems; facilitated training in menu planning as well as food and beverage marketing.
- • Instructed Tips, ServSafe Sanitation Certification, and Guest Satisfaction Seminars.

1986–90

Boston Hilton Hotel • Boston, MA
Director of Food & Beverage (1988–90; promotion)
Managed entire Food and Beverage department of four-diamond hotel comprising two restaurants (including one of downtown Boston's finest upscale restaurants), lounge, night club, retail bake shop, kosher kitchen, and room service.

SUE SENTELL, FMP

Page Two

PROFESSIONAL EXPERIENCE

Boston Hilton Hotel *(cont'd.)*
Hired, trained, and managed staff of 125. Facility included 410 elegant guest rooms as well as 32,000 sq. ft. of meeting space. Annual food/beverage revenues exceeded $5 million.

Beverage Manager (1986–88)

1984–86   **Copenhagen Airport Hotel** • Copenhagen, Denmark
Restaurant Manager
Managed the *Count Dane* restaurant and grillroom.

1981–84   **Hotel des Paris** • Paris, France
Restaurant/Banquet Manager
Managed the *Escoffier* restaurant as well as the banquet department.

1978–81   *Hotel Apprentice* at such fine European hotels as the London Hilton in England, the Cunard Hotel Paris in France, and Holiday Inn Venice in Italy.

EDUCATION

- ■ **Klesheim Hotel School, University of Salzburg** • Saltzburg, Austria
  Institute of Tourism and Hotel Management
  Diploma in Hotel Management (1981 Graduate) — Scholarship Recipient

- ■ **Kilburn Polytechnic** • London, England
  Diploma in Home Economics and Catering (1978 Graduate)
  - • Certificate in Cookery for the Catering Industry (awarded by The Hotel Catering Institutional Management Association of London); Certificate in Cooks Professional (awarded by the National Council of Home Economics, London)

PROFESSIONAL CERTIFICATIONS

- • **The Educational Foundation of the National Restaurant Association**
  FMP — Food Service Management Professional (1994)
- • **Cornell University** • Ithaca, NY
  Professional Development Program — Front Office Management Certification — Concierge Management Certification — Food Service Management Certification
- • **Certified Tips Trainer — Certified Food Service Sanitation Trainer**
- • Successfully completed numerous continuing professional education seminars conducted by Hilton Hotel Corporation and Marriott Hotel Corporation (including Priority One Guest Satisfaction Program, Performance for Excellence, Yes I Can)

AFFILIATIONS

- • **American Hotel and Motel Association**
- • **National Restaurant Association**
- • **Global Hoteliers Club**

Randy Zanassi
1135 Michigan Avenue
East Lansing, MI 48823
(517) 555-0588

QUALIFICATIONS

- Marketing Degree from Michigan State University
- Tom Hopkins Seminar Attendee
- 2 years' experience selling telephone service and publishing materials
- High level of ambition to begin career

EDUCATION

Michigan State University
East Lansing, Michigan   March 1999
Earned a bachelor of arts in Marketing in under the prescribed four-year
course schedule, while financing my own education. My final two years I
was totally self-supporting, working an average of thirty hours per week.

Tom Hopkins Seminar
Detroit, Michigan   February 10, 1999
The seminar "How to Master the Art of Selling" shall improve my
inherent sales abilities. Learning various personnel skills for applicable
situations will be an invaluable asset to my career.

WORK EXPERIENCE

United Parcel Service, Lansing, Michigan   November 1997 to present
Working at UPS enabled me to earn enough to support myself in school. I
earned over $12,000 per year, an impressive accomplishment for a college
student. As well, I maintained the highest production average at our
Center.

Sprint Telephone Division, Lansing, Michigan   1996
Sold local telephone feature services to the consumer market in Lansing.
This experience paved the way for my future career path in sales. After
three months at Sprint, I was the sales leader among the part-time college
students and enjoyed the interaction with the customer. The only reason I
left was to move on to UPS, where the part-time earning potential was
greater.

American Collegiate Marketing, Lansing, Michigan   1995
This position was my introduction to sales, where I worked in a call center
selling magazine subscriptions. Though I enjoyed the sales environment,
my desire was to sell closer to customer in a more direct manner.

SKILLS / INTERESTS

Beyond my formal education, I have a working knowledge of MS Word,
Excel, Outlook and Explorer. I also enjoy playing golf, tennis and fishing.

EMAIL RESUME

```
Renee Christian
2724 Cameron Street
Washington, DC 20008
W (703) 555-1212, H (202) 555-1212
renee.christian@mail.argi.net
```

EXPERIENCE

```
A.T. Kearney - EDS Management Consulting Services
Washington, DC
Principal, 1996 - present
Senior Manager, 1994-1996
```

Specialized in the development of business plans for emerging wireline and wireless telecommunications companies. Responsible for client relationship management and sales into pre-existing client base. Responsible for managing large (up to 30 people) work teams. Provided advice to senior management on a broad variety of strategic and operational subjects, including:
-Business strategy and planning
-Financial modeling
-Competitive assessment
-Market segmentation
-Operations design and optimization
-Mergers and acquisitions
-Implementation assistance
-Churn management

```
Deloitte & Touche Management Consulting
Washington, DC
Manager, 1993-1994
Senior Consultant, 1991-1993
```

Primarily focused on developing market entry strategies for telecommunications clients. Developed very strong financial modeling skills. Responsible for managing smaller projects and developing client deliverables.

EDUCATION

```
B.S. in Physics, Montana State University, 1989
MBA in Finance, Carnegie Mellon University, 1991
```

PUBLICATIONS / SPEECHES

"An Ice Age is Coming to the Wireless World: A Perspective on the Future of Mobile Telephony in the United States," 1995
Thought Leadership Series, EDS Management Consulting

Presented at over two dozen industry conferences, workshops, and panels

ELIZABETH R. FAIRCHILD

5903 13th Street NE, #1617
St. Paul, Minnesota 55232

Home: (606) 555-0234
Office: (714) 555-0982

MANAGEMENT PROFILE

Distinguished management career developing business systems, processes and organizational infrastructures that have improved productivity, increased efficiency, enhanced quality and strengthened financial results. Expertise in identifying and capitalizing on opportunities to enhance corporate image, expand market penetration and build strong operations. Broad-based general management, financial management and project management qualifications. Outstanding record in personnel training, development and leadership.

- Strategic Planning & Tactical Execution
- Business & Performance Reengineering

- Productivity & Efficiency Improvement
- Leadership Development & Career Pathing

PROFESSIONAL EXPERIENCE

NORTHWEST AIRLINES, St. Paul, Minnesota

1977 to Present

Fast-track promotion throughout 20+ year tenure transcending from field to corporate operations in both start-up and large-scale business locations. Built successful business partnerships, managed cross-functional communications, and designed/implemented proactive organizational development, employee performance and corporate culture programs. Key projects and achievements have included:

Start-Up & High-Growth Operations Management

- Held full decision-making responsibility for the daily operations of the St. Paul facility, Northwest's largest center. Led the operation through a period of significant growth, market expansion and diversification including several mergers, divestitures and volume increases.
- Introduced cost management, conflict resolution and corporate culture change initiatives for the start-up Yellowstone operation (1000 personnel and 65 flights daily). Resolved long-standing communication issues, streamlined systems, and created a highly-successful and profitable operation.

Business Process Reengineering

- Orchestrated a complete reengineering of the Ramp Tower operation supporting seven major facilities nationwide. Designed/implemented programs to streamline processes, increase performance and decision-making authority, and position the operation as a cooperative business partner with core operations. Program is currently being implemented throughout Northwest's U.S. operations.
- Spearheaded complete automation of all administrative functions for 6500-employee St. Paul operation. Significantly improved the timeliness and accuracy of key operating, customer and financial information.

Employee Development, Communications & Liaison Affairs

- Created and currently facilitating a corporate-wide conflict management course for 1500 front-line managers in the Airport Customer Service Division.
- Authored a comprehensive operations manual addressing management practices, leadership development, employee evaluation and numerous other organizational issues. Manual was adopted as the corporate standard for all service operations.
- Led integration of more than 150 personnel, all systems and processes into the St. Paul station following Northwest's acquisition of Midwestern Airlines. Completed transition in less than six months with virtually no interruption to service.
- Introduced a series of training programs for over 1500 new and existing personnel. Achieved measurable improvements in employee productivity, operational performance and customer service/satisfaction.

ELIZABETH R. FAIRCHILD

Security, Safety & Inspection Systems, Emergency Preparedness & Crisis Management

- Appointed by corporate committee, following significant public and government scrutiny of the airline industry, to design an emergency preparedness program encompassing more than 600 flights per day and 60% of total St. Paul airport traffic. Program was unanimously approved by Northwest executive management, the FAA, and the Cities of St. Paul and Minneapolis.
- Created a unique program to effectively manage operations during periods of volatility due to both major and minor incidents/delays (e.g., crashes, inclement weather, mechanical problems). Provided employees with a strategic guideline for effective management of customer service and operations. Greatly reduced the number of customer complaints and costs incurred due to cancelled/missed flights.
- Worked with the Director of the St. Paul operation to design and implement a safety and inspection process. Achieved the lowest number of FAA non-compliance findings in the entire corporation.

Career Progression

Northwest Express Yellowstone Manager (1997 to Present)
St. Paul Ramp Tower Manager (1996 to 1997)
Lead Customer Services Agent (1984 to 1988)
Senior Customer Services Agent (1979 to 1984)

EDUCATION

UNIVERSITY OF MINNESOTA

Candidate for Doctoral Degree in Community Psychology, 1995 to Present
Emphasis in Organizational, Sociological & Psychodynamic Theory/Application

Bachelor of Science in Psychology & Sociology, 1995
Magna Cum Laude Graduate; Phi Kappa Phi Honor Society; Golden Key National Honor Society
Outstanding Scholarship Award; State College Scholastic Achievement Award

PERSONAL PROFILE

Professional Affiliations

Northwest Airlines Corporate Mentoring Program
International Airline Women's Association
Society for Community Research & Action
Northwest Airlines Station Manager's Association

Community Affairs

Twin Cities Memorial Hospital Rape Counseling Center
Habitat for Humanity

Research/Publications

Employee Absenteeism
On-The-Job Injuries & Accidents

Ariel S. Conroy 212 · 555 · 5555
10 West 25th Street, Apt. B • New York, NY 10001

Event Planning • Public Relations • Media

High-energy, background in fast-paced corporate event planning, promotion, and media relations / production. Possess outstanding cross-industry skills, superior presentation abilities, a passion for excellence, and a contagious enthusiasm. Tenacious and resourceful; will work any hours necessary and will always find a way to get project done on-time / on-budget.

Summary of Qualifications

- Blend creative and administrative abilities to coordinate unique corporate affairs, and media meeting planning for Dun & Bradstreet, Canadian Imperial Bank (CIB), and Jump-Start Productions.

- Manage budgets; select event venues; handle bookings, travel planning, entertainment, and gift selection. Team with design groups to create event ads and collateral materials.

- Function as associate producer on commercials, and as media marketer for Jump-Start Productions, a television / cable commercial production firm. Maintain excellent rapport with producers, clients, and high-profile talent.

- Highly experienced in PC word processing, database / spreadsheet design, and presentation development. Familiar with Mac programs.

Career Highlights

- Helped plan and deliver Dun & Bradstreet's largest and most luxurious special event, a $1 million golf / spa outing at Pebble Beach, CA that was attended by nearly three hundred top clients, executives, and their guests.

- Coordinated cocktail receptions, luncheons, company tours, and interviewing rounds for D&B's recruiting events. Created sophisticated spreadsheets to organize hundreds of participants into six $100 thousand events.

- Planned high-profile golf and entertainment excursions and closing dinners for CIIB. Coordinated cocktails, dinner menus and locations, transportation, executive suite at Madonna concert, and other entertainment. Purchased amenity gifts, inspected sites and paid invoices.

Professional Development

PUBLIC RELATIONS AND EVENTS COORDINATOR Dun & Bradstreet, New York, NY	1996 to present
MEDIA MARKETING REPRESENTATIVE (freelance) Jump-Start Productions, Inc., New York, NY	1994 to present
SPECIAL EVENTS COORDINATOR / PROJECT ASSISTANT Canadian Imperial Bank, New York, NY	1991 to 1995

Education

Bachelor of Arts in Communications, Queens College, Flushing, NY, 1990

**Areas of
Expertise**

corporate representation

PR strategies

press releases

presentations

conflict mediation

investor relations

consumer relations

event coordination

budget development

travel planning

meeting planning

venue selection

cocktail receptions

luncheons / dinners

entertainment selection

golf outings

theme design

invitations

corporate gift selection

collateral materials

vendor payment

Jessamyn Swanson   Writer

Professional Profile

Extensive background in written communication and editorial administration.

Write a weekly small-business feature for Newsday, the country's seventh largest newspaper.

Serve as assistant editor and regularly contribute topical articles for the lifestyle magazine Prestige.

Develop and pitch story concepts, land the interview, do the research, and get the job done on time.

Writer

cover stories, features, essays, interviews, film and music reviews, sports, fiction, poetry, plays

Editor

content, editorial board management, production, final copy edit, deadlines

Interviewer

newsmakers, politicians, entertainers, human interest

Career Development

ASSISTANT EDITOR AND FEATURE WRITER

Prestige Magazine, a Times-Mirror Publication, Melville, NY 1994 to present

Handle multiple responsibilities using excellent writing, editing and time-management skills. Conduct general copy editing and reporter interface on a routine basis. Assign stories, development, set-up contracts, and establish deadlines for fifteen free-lance writers and contributing editors.

Generate story ideas, conduct interviews, research and write full-length features, Q&A format articles, and celebrity, business and social profiles. Have interviewed Chevy Chase, Bernadette Castro, Jim McCann, Christy Brinkley, Bob Wallach, Robert Klein, Liz Smith, Donna Karan, Alan King, Carolyn McCarthy, Shirley Strum Kenny, Carol Baldwin, and Mario Buatta among others.

WEEKLY SMALL BUSINESS FEATURE Writer

Newsday, Melville, NY   1996 to present

Seek out and research potential businesses, pitch ideas to editor, and stay two weeks ahead of deadline. Maintain diversity of profiles and relate content to current business, political or social events.

Have profiled over 100 businesses since the feature's debut. Originally approached by Newsday to write one article; assignment developed into a weekly profile of unusual entrepreneurial businesses. One of only a few free-lancers to maintain a Newsday business section weekly feature.

Education and Activities

Bachelor of Arts, in English, The State University of New York at Stony Brook, 1992

Jessamyn Swanson   10 First St., Patchogue, NY 11772   (516) 555-5555   JAS@aol.com

INDEXES

Alphabetical Listing of Cover Letters

Index by Industry/Job Title

General Index

ABOUT THE AUTHORS

Jay Block, CPRW (Certified Professional Resume Writer), is the contributing cofounder of the Professional Association of Resume Writers (PARW). As the official organization governing resume standards, PARW aims to elevate the skills of resume professionals and provides the only certification process for resume writers. Mr. Block helped develop the PARW national certification process and is a widely respected national speaker, author, and career coach.

Michael Betrus, CPRW, is the author of *The Guide to Executive Recruiters* (McGraw-Hill), the most comprehensive directory of its kind.

Jay Block and Michael Betrus are co-authors of the bestsellers *101 Best Resumes* and *101 More Best Resumes*.